Observing the Other: Writings in Psychoanalysis, Psychotherapy, and Psychiatry

Observing the Other:
Writings in Psychoanalysis, Psychotherapy, and Psychiatry

by Peter J. Buckley

IPBOOKS.net
International Psychoanalytic Books

International Psychoanalytic Books (IPBooks)
New York • http://www.IPBooks.net

Observing the Other: Writings in Psychoanalysis, Psychotherapy, and Psychiatry

Published by IPBooks, Queens, NY
Online at: www.IPBooks.net

ISBN: 978-1-956864-76-2

For Remy and Sasha

Heartfelt thanks to:

Jacob Arlow, Harold Bourne, Marc Galanter, Mary-Joan Gerson,
Philip Herschenfeld, Edward Hornick, Byram Karasu,
Frederic Kass, Salvatore Lomonaco, Robert Michels,
Leo Spiegel, William Tucker, Judy Yanof, Joseph Youngerman

CONTENTS

A Journey

For some fifty years, I have been privileged to practice and teach both psychiatry and psychoanalysis. While the two disciplines are separate entities, they mirror and inform one another. Both have undergone radical changes since I embarked on my professional training as a psychiatric resident in the late 1960's and as a psychoanalytic candidate in the early 1970s.

The changes in the psychiatric landscape have been revolutionary. These include the refinement of phenomenological psychiatric diagnoses in DSM-3 and subsequent DSM revisions, an increasing biological basis for understanding the somatic origins of mental illness and effective pharmacological treatments, the expansion of psychodynamic thinking beyond ego psychology to incorporate differing theoretical perspectives, and a dramatic shift in socio-cultural attitudes toward the clinician-patient relationship (Buckley, Michels, & Mackinnon, 2006).

Radical changes have simultaneously taken place in the theory and practice of psychoanalysis in the United States. The previously dominant clinical model of ego psychology, with its emphasis on ubiquitous unconscious conflict between instinctual drives and the demands of reality and conscience, all mediated by the ego, is now but one of an array of differing theoretical views which include object relations, self psychology and their off-shoots, the relational and intersubjective models. All these insurgent frames of dynamic mental functioning have significant implications for psychoanalytic technique and our understanding of the nature of therapeutic change.

Throughout my academic and clinical career, I have been witness to these seismic changes. Thus the papers and essays in this volume are a reflection of my personal intellectual and clinical journey through this evolving terrain.

I was fortunate enough to undertake my psychiatric training at Albert Einstein College of Medicine in the Bronx. Under the inspired leadership of the first Chair of the Department of Psychiatry, Milton Rosenbaum, the residency program at Jacobi Hospital was an epicenter of progressive teaching and practice. Innovative treatment methods such as the day-hospital for the severely mentally ill alongside family and group therapies. the Tavistock-derived "therapeutic community" all accompanied by a continuous dialogue and debate among faculty and students concerning "best" treatment methods for disparate patients. This "university" provided a remarkable education and was imbued with humanism and embraced the Roman playwright Terance's credo: "I am human and nothing human is alien to me. "

My psychoanalytic training took place at The New York Psychoanalytic Institute in the early 1970's. At the time, NYPI was an intellectually-rigorous bastion of ego psychology with a superb and brilliant faculty. The formal training at NYPI was excellent albeit I was skeptical of its conservative ideology which catalyzed a life-long interest in object relations theory (Buckley, 1986).

In my academic life and clinical practice I have been perpetually intrigued by the question of what are the actual elements that facilitate positive psychological change. This "mystery" led me to some research endeavors whose results suggested that the therapeutic relationship accompanied by a positive transference was the bedrock upon which "neurotic misery is turned into normal human unhappiness" (Buckley, Conte, et al. , 1984, 1981).

As Leo Stone commented on the repeat analyses that he conducted: "one of the things that struck me most was how little people remember of interpretive material—the basic affective relationship between the two persons so dominated the actual responses that this other (interpretive process) seemed unimportant to them" (Raymond & Rosbrow-Reich, 1997).

Jacob Arlow commented: "like the creative writer, the analyst is influenced by the evocative power of the experience with other people" (Raymond & Rosbrow-Reich, 1997).

Thus, in the choice of a career as a psychiatrist and psychoanalyst, one can see the parallel to what Wordsworth said about the poet's art:

"It is a homage paid to the native and naked dignity of man, to the grand elementary principle of pleasure, by which he knows, and feels and lives, and moves. We have no sympathy but what is propagated by pleasure; I would not be misunderstood, but whenever we sympathize with pain, it will be found that the sympathy is produced and carried on by subtle combinations with pleasure."

REFERENCES

Buckley, P.J., Michels, R., Mackinnon, R.A. (2006). Changes in the psychiatric landscape. *American Journal of Psychiatry* 163:757–760.

Buckley, P., ed, (1986). *Essential Papers on Object Relations. New York:* New York University Press.

——— Conte, H.R., Plutchik, R., Wild, K.V. & Karasu, T.B. (1984). Psychodynamic variables as predictors of psychotherapy outcome. *American Journal of Psychiatry* 14(6):742–748.

Conte H. R., Buckley, P., Picard, S, Karasu, T.B. (1994). Relations between satisfaction with therapists and psychotherapy outcome. *Journal of Psychotherapy, Practice and Research.* 3:215–221.

——— Karasu, T.B., Charles, E. (1981). Psychotherapists view their personal therapy. *Psychotherapy: Theory, Research and Practice.* Volume 18(3):299–305.

Raymond L.W., Rosbrow-Reich, S. (1997). *The Inward eye. Psychoanalysts Reflect on Their Lives and Work.* The Analytic Press: Hillsdale, NJ/ London, pp. 124 & 61.

Wordsworth, W. (1802). From *Lyrical Ballads with Other Poems.* In: preface to the second edition of *Major British Writers, Enlarged Edition,* p.23, New York: Harcourt Brace & Company, 1959.

SECTION ONE: CASE STUDIES

CHAPTER 1

The Empty Album

There is no good father, that's the rule. Don't lay the blame on men but on the bond of paternity, which is rotten. To beget children, nothing better; to have them, what iniquity! Had my father lived, he would have lain on me at full length and would have crushed me. As luck had it, he died young. Amidst Aeneas and his fellows who carry their Anchises on their backs, I move from shore to shore, alone and hating those invisible begetters who bestraddle their sons all their lives long.
—Jean-Paul Sartre

Shortly after Sartre's birth, his father died of intestinal fever contracted in Indo-China. In his autobiography, Sartre (1981) extolls the virtues of being fatherless, yet the passage quoted above (Sartre, 1981, p. 19) provides a glimpse of his true feelings and fantasies concerning the father he never knew. The vicissitudes of psychological development when one parent is lost are manifold and contingent upon many variables, including the constitutional capacities of the child, but there is a general consensus that such a loss must have deleterious effects. Anna Freud and Burlingham (1944), in their study of children without fathers during World War II, found intense and persistent attachments to a fantasized father. Neubauer (1960) in a case study of the effects of paternal parental absence on a girl during the oedipal phase of development found no evidence of serious pathology. However, a developmental deficiency was noted in this child, deriving from her not having lived through and mastered the oedipal conflict. Neubauer observed, "When a parent is absent, there is an absence of oedipal reality. The absent parent becomes endowed with magical power either to gratify or to punish" (p. 308).

Ross (1979) in a review of psychoanalytic contributions on paternity noted that, until recently, the father has been a relatively forgotten parent in the psychoanalytic developmental literature. He has highlighted the father's active, positive role in the child's preoedipal development, and states, "it is the father who first offers ways out of a child's arresting entanglement with the mother." Ross has underlined the child's need for a father with whom to identify. He views the father, through his position as the first significant other outside the mother-child dyad, as inviting independent expression by the infant and serving as mediator between mother and child, thus preparing the way for further development.

In this paper a clinical example will be presented of the effects of the absence of the father during the childhood of a male analysand, in particular, its consequences for his later object choice. While this patient confirms the importance of the father in the child's development, the presentation of this case has a more central objective. In essence, this patient is an "experiment of nature" who provides a clinical test of object-relations theory.

Object-relations theorists postulate that early object relations determine the nature of later object choice. As an example, Bak (1973) has argued that "'being in love'—is based on undoing the separation of mother and child" (p. 6) and that the adult condition of being in love draws imagery and sensations from early ego phases of the infant. Similarly, the vicissitudes of early object relations have been invoked to explain the psychopathology of serious disorders, including the borderline states (Shapiro, 1978). Pathological phenomena seen in borderline states such as splitting and projective identification (and the consequent stormy quality of interpersonal relations) are viewed as the persistence into adulthood of primitive defenses due to the failure of the development of object constancy (Kernberg, 1975). This latter failure is ascribed to the pathological nature of early object relations which can be regressively reactivated in adulthood (for instance, in the transference) in patients suffering from borderline conditions.

Ogden (1983) has stated that object-relations theory is fundamentally a theory of unconscious internal object relations in dynamic interplay with current interpersonal experience. He has further proposed that the establishment of an internal object relationship "requires a dual splitting of the ego into a pair of dynamically unconscious suborganizations of personality, one identified with the self and the other with the object in the original early object relationship. These aspects of ego stand in a particular relationship to one another the nature of which is *determined by the infant's subjective experience of the early relationship*" (p. 239). He further posits that "the internal object relationship may be later reexternalized by means of projection and projective identification in an interpersonal setting thus generating the transference and countertransference phenomena of analysis and all other interpersonal interactions" (p. 221).

This is not a theoretical position universally held by all object-relations theorists. For instance, Kernberg (1974a), (1974b), (1977), (1980) has examined love relations from the viewpoint of object-relations theory. His propositions are more broadly based than those of object-relations theorists who state that earliest object relations determine later object choice. He suggests that the capacity to fall in love and remain in love reflects the successful completion of two developmental stages: the first requiring that lack of integration of the self and object representation be overcome in the context of establishing ego identity and the capacity for object relations, the second requiring "the successful overcoming of oedipal conflicts and related unconscious prohibitions against a full sexual relationship" (Kernberg, 1974a, p. 486). Thus, Kernberg has suggested that it is not simply the external person who is internalized as an object.

The reductionism involved in the view that early object relations determine later object choice has been questioned by Arlow (1980), who has demonstrated that the nature of adult object choice is dependent on an interrelation of identification, defense, object relations, and instinctual gratification. He has drawn attention to the central importance of unconscious fantasy in every love relationship. In his view, it is the unconscious fantasy derived from the early vicissitudes of drive and object experience that determines patterns of loving and the specific types of persons that will correspond to the object choice.

The case example to be presented here will demonstrate the manner in which the particular experience in childhood of the absence of the father became connected with drive and development in such a way that an unconscious fantasy was established which profoundly influenced later object choice. For this patient it was not simply the experience of an absent father that determined later object choice, but the development of a mental representation of the lost father cathected with sexual and aggressive drives which were organized around a persistent set of unconscious fantasy wishes. It was this complex configuration that influenced later object choice. Until this patient's mother remarried when he was five, there was no base of object relations with a father figure in reality. Nevertheless, as will be shown, the patient developed an object concept in his fantasy which determined subsequent interactions with his stepfather, authority figures, and even with several of his girl friends.

This case illustrates the fallacy of ascribing to the experience of early object relations alone the dominant role in later object choice, and the necessity of taking into account the influence of the drives and intrapsychic development on object choice in adulthood. This patient's analysis also shows the central role of the Oedipus complex in integrating the many determinants of object choice, including those derived from earlier stages of development. Finally, this patient provided a further opportunity for the analytic investigation of what Anna Freud and Dann (1951) have entitled "experiments provided by fate."

CLINICAL MATERIAL

The analytic case I shall discuss is of a man who first came for treatment at the age of twenty-seven, complaining of feelings of depression subsequent to the recent break-up of a love affair. Although he was good-looking and articulate, there was a wistful, understated quality about his manner of describing himself and his life. He was the only child of his mother's first marriage and was born and raised in a Protestant household in the midwest. When he was six months old, his father abandoned him and his mother, and the patient had no contact with his father subsequently. He did not know why his parents' marriage had disintegrated, though he had some vague idea, resulting from his mother's comments, that his natural father was unable to tolerate the responsibilities of parenthood. He had never pursued this subject with his mother in order to obtain further clarification. He did know something about his father's family, however, since his paternal grandfather was a wealthy merchant banker.

The patient was raised by his mother and his maternal grandmother, who lived nearby. When he was five, his mother remarried. His half-sister was a product of this marriage. He recalled how involved he had been with her when she was a baby. He assisted his mother in diapering and feeding his infant half-sister. He remembered many episodes of his babysitting while his mother was seeing her psychiatrist. He related that she had begun psychotherapy shortly after his halfsister's birth for what he thought was depression, though this, too, like many other events in the history of the family, had an unclear quality for him.

At the age of twelve, he agreed to take his stepfather's surname as his own, but he was mortified to discover when he was fourteen that he had not been formally adopted. This peculiar state of affairs was rationalized by his mother and stepfather as being due to their concern that he not be blocked from obtaining an inheritance from his natural father's family, even though they had adamantly opposed his accepting offers of money from his paternal grandparents when he was a teenager. The patient was an excellent student, was admitted to an Ivy League college, and then attended law school. At the time of clinical presentation, he was an associate in a law firm.

His mother he described as a bright, lively woman who was, however, "something of a flake." She was prone to volatile moods. He described her manner of thinking as being analogous to his own: "creative, different," and given to "tangential associations." He had a sneaking admiration for her cognitive style, which he saw as original and stimulating. His stepfather was a successful businessman whom the patient described as being very different from him and his mother. He viewed him as rigid and rather literal-minded in his approach to the world. He complained that his stepfather would never acknowledge feelings. The patient categorized their relationship as ambivalent. He described himself as being very involved with his family, and he placed great emphasis on the virtues of family life and loyalty to the family; but he was bitter in his complaint that he was not "appreciated," especially by his stepfather, for his filial devotion.

The early part of the analysis was dominated by his preoccupation with his ex-girlfriend. A complete rupture had not occurred, and he ruminated at great length about reestablishing their love affair. It gradually emerged that there had been much sadomasochistic behavior on his part towards his girl friend. About a year prior to coming for treatment, he had found his sexual interest in her waning. This reached the point where all sexual activity ceased even though they were living together. Simultaneously, he had had a number of transient affairs with other women, which he made known to his girl friend. The decline in their sexual activities had led to his girl friend's moving out of his apartment. Filled with self-pity and loneliness, he made a number of attempts at reconciliation with her. Once the separation had occurred, his sexual interest returned, but he was then devastated when she told him that his behavior had resulted in her "snapping" and her love for him vanishing. He became obsessed with the need to have her physically present again. His anxiety at being alone was almost overwhelming, and he was preoccupied with "filling up the empty space." The analysis gradually revealed a strong identification with his girl friend. She was an adopted child who had been abandoned by her natural parents and, like her, he saw himself as an abandoned child. His mistreatment of her and the separation from her brought into consciousness a view of himself as being just like his biological father, someone who walked out the door leaving a helpless infant behind.

During this early phase of the analysis, he became preoccupied with what he viewed as similarities between himself and his biological father. He felt that he, too, was a "bad seed," that he had genetically inherited a capacity for irresponsibility and destructive behavior. He saw himself as being like Heathcliff, the abandoned child, spurned in love, and capable of revengeful destructive behavior. An unconscious sense of criminality gradually became increasingly prominent. This was based on an identification with his biological father's action of leaving him. For the patient, his own criminal propensities were confirmed by his behavior toward his girl friend.

As his anxiety diminished over what was now an irrevocable separation from his girl friend, he became involved with other women, but much of his behavior was marked by hostility and barely suppressed murderous anger. A brief sexual liaison with a woman whom he consciously liked and admired led to his abruptly and arbitrarily breaking off all contact with her as soon as she expressed feelings of love for him. This sudden abandonment of the relationship was a further acting out of his identification with his natural father. His biological father, even in his physical absence, had been a powerful force in his mental life. A mental representation of him with two sides, negative and positive, had evolved which became an integral part of the patient. The former was manifest in the patient's belief that he, too, was an abandoner, a mistreater of women and a potential failure as a parent. His stepfather's admonitions were warranted, he was a bad seed, a criminal just like his natural father.

At this stage of the analysis the patient began to realize how grateful he had been to his stepfather for coming into the family and making everything "normal." He now recollected many memories of how he had seen himself and his fatherless family as "weird" in comparison to the other children in the community where he lived as a small boy. This sense of being unusual, different, and an exception, had given rise to a profound sense of entitlement which manifested itself early in the analysis through acting out in the form of many missed sessions. The conviction of guilt concerning his girl friend and the women with whom he had subsequently had affairs.

The second phase of the analysis revolved around his involvement with older men, in particular senior partners in his law firm. He was convinced he had a special relationship with them, that he brought something crucial into their lives, a new way of experiencing the world. He would be provocative and teasing with them, imagining he was creative and providing them with a new perspective on life. He would then be surprised and disillusioned when they became angry at his teasing and attacked him. Gradually the analysis revealed the fixity of this pattern of behavior with older men. Behind it lay an unconscious wish to submit to them, to engage them sexually by verbally sparring and then to accept their attacks passively. At this stage, it became apparent that the paradigm for this type of involvement was his relationship with his stepfather whom, as a child, he would frequently provoke. He remembered his stepfather hitting him full in the face when pushed to the limit. As a little boy he had the fantasy that his stepfather was doing this to beat his biological father out of him. Unconsciously, these episodes with his stepfather represented a form of sexual congress. The constant longings for the absent father that he had experienced up until the age of five were answered by the arrival on the scene of his stepfather. His love for him was profound. His early years spent with his mother had led to a strong identification with her, and he had been intensely jealous of the fact that she slept with his stepfather. He had found his own form of intimacy with him through constant battles. Through all of this, however, there was a sense of unrequited love expressed in his firm conviction that his stepfather did not fully appreciate him and would never tell him how much he loved him. This feeling of not being appreciated resonated with his experience of being abandoned.

As this material emerged in the analysis, the patient became conscious of a rekindled wish to see his biological father, a wish that had been almost constantly present during his early life. Gradually this became stronger, and fantasies of a happy reunion and reconciliation came into play. The fantasy surfaced that perhaps it had not been all his natural father's fault that he had been abandoned; perhaps his mother had a lot to do with it; maybe it was alright to be like him. the positive, idealized side of his fantasies concerning his natural father became conscious—that his father, like him, questioned the "ordinary" way of living and that his leaving the patient and his mother had been precipitated by a need not to succumb to the conventional. In short, his natural father, like the patient's view of himself, was an original, an iconoclast, someone who could transcend convention. The idealized image of the lost father was again dominant in his mental life, resurrected by his feelings of disappointment about his stepfather's refusal to acknowledge him. Within the transference at this stage, he felt the analyst did not appreciate him or fully understand him and was letting him down by not providing "direction."

The urge to see his natural father became irresistible and, with some effort, the patient tracked him down and arranged to meet him. This meeting was a devastating experience. His biological father wanted to talk only about his own problems, his sense of aimlessness and the fact that life had not treated him as well as it might have. He seemed to have little interest in his son. The patient bitterly exclaimed, "The real disappointment was that he showed up." The reality was drastically incongruent with the internal fantasy. His natural father was not the powerful trampler of convention, he was weak, mean-spirited, and a failure.

The patient had a series of associations at this juncture in which he complained of the empty photograph album—there were no baby pictures of him in his home though there were hundreds of his half-sister. He had not known what his biological father looked like because there were no pictures of him, but he had had an unconscious image of him and had now been bitterly disappointed. His stepfather and the older men whom he had admired and with whom he had had such acrimonious relationships had all partly fit this idealized image of his biological father.

Disappointed by the revelations of this dramatic meeting, the patient embarked on an attempt at psychological restitution of the shattered image of the lost father. He fell in love with an attractive young woman who was assertive, ambitious, and self-confident. She, like his stepfather, was an executive in the business world. Within a short time of meeting her, he proposed marriage to her.

It quickly became apparent that, unconsciously, she represented his stepfather and ultimately the idealized lost father. Her assertive qualities had appealed to him for that very reason. As relevant dream material was brought into the analysis and pointed in this direction, the patient began to act out more and more. When the unconscious meaning of his impulsive wish to marry this woman was interpreted to him, he abruptly terminated the analysis, unable to tolerate the bringing into consciousness of his wish to submit and be sexually penetrated. My interpretations were seen as assaultive, castrating, and directly frightening in their own right. His rationalization for this sudden decision was that he needed to be "independent" and make decisions for himself. This flew in the face of the emerging evidence in the analysis of a powerful instinctual urge to reconstitute the shattered mental representation of the lost father through his marriage.

Eighteen months later, the patient returned to analysis. In the interim, he had married, but marriage had proved, inevitably, to be a disappointment. His wife could not satisfy his longings for union with the idealized lost father. He was now in an obsessional crisis concerning an imminent decision over whether or not he should accept a position that had been offered to him in another law firm. He vacillated back and forth, experiencing paroxysms of anguish at the thought of leaving his current firm where, through dint of creative work on his part, he had established himself as a respected and well-thought-of young attorney. It quickly became clear that the primary psychological issue again involved an older man, a senior partner in his firm. This man, of an ascetic and extremely formal disposition, had become the emotional center of the patient's psychological life for at least a year prior to his returning to analysis. The previous pattern had been repeated—a desperate need to be appreciated as special, original, and talented by this man had forced him into a sadomasochistic involvement with him. Enraged at his inability to elicit the required response to his provocations, the patient in a fury had sought and easily obtained another prestigious position. Now, faced with leaving this man's firm, he was in a panic. Analytic connections between this relationship and his longing for the lost father were easily made and resulted in a dissipation of his anxiety. Associations to a dream of reunion and an experience of an epiphany revealed that one unconscious element in his returning to analysis was the fantasy of reuniting with the lost father through the person of the analyst.

The patient took his new position and then had a dream of seeing his mother standing on the floor of an amphitheater where she was sprayed with small white flags that stuck to her body. These flags appeared to have names on them, but he could not make out what they were. His associations led him to see that his own name remained in question. The flags were small and white and reminded him of spermatozoa. His mother was being impregnated, but whose name was on the sperm? What was his real name? This dream became a catalyst for thoughts about his own fatherhood and an awareness of how much he wanted to have a son whom he would nurture, raise, and never abandon.

An apparent rapprochement occurred with his stepfather during this period. However, during the course of one of their meetings, his stepfather stated that his involvement in raising the patient had only derived from his sense of duty and responsibility to the patient's mother. He further underlined this by complaining that it could be many years before he was a grandfather implying that any children his stepson might have would not be regarded as his grandchildren. This stark revelation evoked much pain and anger and left the patient with a "large cavity" in his heart. (Early in the analysis, he had recalled the period before his stepfather came on the scene as being one where "I had a hole in my heart.") Shortly after these events, he had a dream in which an older man was making love to his wife in front of his eyes. During the course of the dream, he was at first enraged, but then he was surprised to observe he no longer cared about what was happening. His long sought-after father had irrevocably left him for another woman. He poignantly stated, "I thought I had two fathers, but now I discover that I have none." A period of grief and mourning of this loss occurred in the analysis. This was followed by intensification of the powerful wish to have a child. At first conflictual, this became an increasingly strong desire. Analytic work revealed that within the wish to have a child lay a true solution to his quest. He would find a father by becoming a father to his son and would identify with his own child in the fathering he himself provided.

DISCUSSION

Meissner (1979) has commented that the current theory of object relations inevitably leads directly to the problem of the relation between what is internal and what is external. He states that "there is a supposition in the object relations view of development that the patterning of intra-psychic development depends on the sequence and quality of the infant's object experience" (p. 346). McDevitt (1979) has argued that the outcome of the internalizations that lead to a mental representation of the object will depend both on the child's endowment and, what is important for this paper, the actual nature of the parent-child interaction. The contemporary theory of object relations thus places great emphasis on the direct experience in reality of the object, especially the parents, by the child, in short that the child's earliest actual object relations are determinative of later interpersonal reactions.

In developing the concept of the object, Freud (1905) postulated that libido is concentrated upon objects, "becoming fixed upon them or abandoning them, ... moving from one object to another and, from these situations, directing the subject's sexual activity, which leads to the satisfaction, that is, to the partial and temporary extinction, of the libido" (p. 217). A central element of Freud's conceptualization of the object is that the mental representation of the thing or person is cathected with libidinal energy and not the external thing or person. As Arlow (1980) has pointed out, the failure to maintain this definition has led to considerable confusion in the use of the term object, in particular the tendency to use the terms interpersonal relations and object relations as if they were identical. Arlow has commented that "fundamentally, it is the effect of unconscious fantasy wishes, connected with specific mental representations of objects that colors, distorts and affects the ultimate quality of interpersonal relations. It is important to distinguish between the person and the object. This is essentially the core of transference, in which the person in the real world is confused with a mental representation of the childhood object, a mental representation of what was either a person or a thing" (p. 114). Arlow has thus emphasized the concept of the object as an intrapsychic mental representation whose evolution cannot be separated from the vicissitudes of the drives. He has stated "in later experience these [drives] become organized in terms of persistent unconscious fantasies that ultimately affect object choice and patterns of loving" (p. 109). Arlow further comments that it is not simply "the experience with the object, but what is done with the experience, that is decisive for development" (p. 129).

The case example presented here supports this thesis. The lost father, symbolized by the absence of photographs, the "empty album," became a strongly cathected mental representation invested with libidinal energy, in Arlow's words, "a persistently 'internal' experience" (p. 113). Unconscious fantasies of the lost father with whom the patient had no contact in reality and longing for him organized the patient's drives and determined his own selfidentity as well as his later object choice.

Arlow has further noted that "in earlier phases the organization of the object concept is under the aegis of the pleasure principle" and that "the fundamental tendency to seek an identity of pleasurable perception goes far in explaining the persistent influence of unconscious childhood fantasies" (p. 117). The prominent negative Oedipus complex in this patient revolved around an autonomously created mental representation of the father without any contact with the person in reality. The appearance of his stepfather on the scene provided a real person for the patient onto whom these libidinal derivatives could be displaced.

An admixture of sexual and aggressive forces under the aegis of the oedipus complex led to the constant repetition of hostile engagement with, and submission to, powerful older paternal substitutes. In each case, he was disappointed and abandoned, playing out repeatedly his unconscious scenario. The resolution of this repetition-compulsion required a libidinal investment of his own capacity for fatherhood, a discovery of the lost father within the self.

A comment should be made on the nature of the urge for reconciliation as seen in this patient. Behind the rekindled desire to meet with his biological father lay an intense wish for reunion and reconciliation. This was based on a fantasy of common identity—he was just like his father and his father resembled him, iconoclastic, a free spirit, creative, and innovative. Based on this fantasy of common identity, the patient felt that, on physically meeting, an immediate empathic rapport would occur between them that would lead to an indissoluble, intimate, sustained relationship that would repair the rupture of the past. Precipitated by his recurrent failures to find this father in the older men with whom he had become sadomasochistically involved, the fantasy of an exact identity between his father and himself that would be automatically revealed fueled his action of contacting him. The bleak reality of who his father was as a living person and the failure to find any psychological congruence with him led to profound disillusionment. While one cannot extrapolate to the whole psychology of reconciliation from this one case, it is conceivable that the development of an unconscious belief in an ultimately common identity of character and purpose with the other is a central component in attempts at reconciliation, and that successful reconciliation requires a partial confirmation in reality of such commonality.

Freud (1921) observed that the little boy manifests "a special interest in his father; he would like to grow like him and be like him ..." (p. 105). In wanting to become and be like him, the patient presented here developed both a positive and a negative identification with the lost father. It must be emphasized, however, that the identification was with a *fantasy object*, not a real one. The patient was making himself like his father, but it was not like any father he knew or with whom he had actual interpersonal relations. The longing for reunion with the fantasized idealized object of the father was answered by the arrival of his stepfather. The identification with the fantasized negative object of the father led to the development of an unconscious sense of criminality and guilt that manifested itself both in provocative behavior toward his stepfather and paternal substitutes, leading to literal and figurative beatings, and his hostile actions toward women. This unconscious sense of criminality has to be seen as arising out of a borrowed sense of guilt. It was his biological father who was guilty of crimes against the patient, but he had never received his just punishment from the world at large. The patient fantasized bringing down upon himself the punishment that should have been meted out to his father. His provocative behavior was unconsciously designed to bring this to pass.

This case also highlights the complex nature of identification. As commonly used in the psychological literature, the term is woefully inadequate and poorly defined, more often than not referring to a simple imitation. Schafer (1968) has explicated in detail the manifold aspects of identifications, and postulated that they are expressions of unconscious fantasies. Consequently, identifications inevitably include drive derivatives, defensive aspects, and superego components. As such, they have to be viewed as amalgams based on actual experience, memory, instinctual wishes, and defenses, all of which form a unity, but it is one that can be regressively dissolved into its component parts. For the patient presented here the identification with the lost father with its separate negative and positive sides possessed all of these elements, but was based on a fantasy object, not an actual object. The identification as a whole could be renounced because the unconscious, instinctually based fantasies of punishment and reunion were brought into consciousness and worked through in the analysis. In a restitutive reaction to the loss of this fundamentally pathological identification was created a new, healthier identity grounded in his own potential paternity.

Arlow (1980) has noted:

> ... *what is later organized and conceptualized as the need-gratifying object originates out of the memories of repetitive sensory impressions accompanied by feelings of gratification. Object seeking is predominantly oriented by the need to try to achieve the identity of pleasurable perceptions remembered but not independently attainable by infants ... Subsequently, the memory traces of pleasurable sensory impressions connected with an external person become organized into a coherent memory structure, a mental representation of a person, which we call "object." The term, object, therefore, represents a concept pertaining to a persistent, that is a structured, experience. In parallel fashion a coherent organization of memory traces of representations connected with pain may serve as the basis for the concept of another kind of object representation. Thus, it happens that two sets of memories of sensory impressions may be organized as mental representations, one associated with pain, the other with pleasure ... It is only later in the course of development that the seemingly disparate mental representations of objects having identical sensory impressions are fused into the concept of an external person whose mental representations psychologically may be vested or associated with memories of pain as well as pleasure [pp. 117–118].*

The case presented here illustrate this development and highlights the need to use a precise term in talking of the object, namely the *mental representation* of the object which may or may not be built up out of experiences with a "real object." Since this patient's mental representation of the object and paternal identification was based on a fantasy object, this case contradicts a central tenet of some object-relations theorists, namely that earliest actual object relations are determinative of later interpersonal reactions.

Ross (1980, unpublished) notes that fatherhood itself can revive a variety of primitive identifications and conflicts from childhood. He observes that producing a child represents an oedipal triumph while simultaneously demanding a renunciation of the longing to be cared for by beneficent, omnipotent parents. Ross also comments that there is a search for a representation of the "good father" with whom a new father can identify. For the patient presented here, traversing these psychological obstacles was greatly compounded by the absence of his father and resultant unconscious fantasies that arose without any contact with the father or father substitute in real life. Yet it was not an insurmountable task.

Sartre (1981), one of the supreme moralists and writers of this century, also found a solution for the absence of his father. He said of his childhood: "I keep creating myself; I am the giver and the gift. If my father were alive, I would know my rights and my duties. He is dead and I am unaware of them" (p. 32). Yet he found substitutes for his dead father: "I began my life as I shall no doubt end it: amidst books" (p. 40). Speaking of the writers of the past who entranced him he said: "I had no brothers and sisters, no playmates, and they [the dead writers] were my first friends. They had loved, and suffered manfully, like the heroes of their novels, and, above all, had triumphed in the end.—In my sight they were not dead; at any rate, not entirely. They had been metamorphosed into books" (p. 64).

REFERENCES

Arlow, J.A. (1980). Object concept and object choice. *Psychoanal. Q.*49: *109–133.*

Bak, R. (1973). Being in love and object loss. *Int. J. Psychoanal.*54:*1–8.*

Freud, A. Burlingham, D. (1944I). *Infants without Families.* New York: Int. Univ. Press.

——— & ——— & Dann, S. (1951). An experiment in group upbringing .*Psychoanal. Study Child.* 6:*127–168.*

Freud, S. (1905). Three essays on sexuality. *S.E.* 7:123–246

——— (1921). Group psychology and the analysis of the ego. *S.E.* 18.

Kernberg, O.F. (1974a). Barriers to falling and remaining in love. *J. Am. Psychoanal. Assoc.* 22:*486–511.*

——— (1974b). Mature love: prerequisites and characteristics. *J. Am. Psychoanal. Assoc.* 22:*743–768.*

——— (1975). *Borderline Conditions and Pathological Narcissism.* New York: Aronson.

——— (1977). Boundaries and structure in love relations. *J. Am. Psychoanal. Assoc.* 25:*81–114.*

——— (1980). Love, the couple, and the group: a psychoanalytic frame .*Psychoanal. Q.*49:*79–108.*

——— (1979). The role of internalization in the development of object relations during the separation-individuation phase. *J. Am. Psychoanal. Assoc.* 27:*327–343.*

Meissner, W.W. (1979). Internalization and object relations .*J. Am. Psychoanal. Assoc.* 27:*345–360.*

Neubauer, P.B. (1960). The one-parent child and his oedipal development. *Psychoanal. Study Child* 15:*286–309.*

Ogden, T.N. (1983). The concept of internal object relations. *Int. J. Psychoanal.*63: *227–241.*

Ross, J.M. (1979). Fathering: a review of some psychoanalytic contributions on paternity. *Int. J. Psychoanal.*60:*318–327.*

Sartre, J.-P. (1981). *The Words.* New York: Vintage Press.

Schafer, R. (1968). *Aspects of Internalization* .New York: Int. Univ. Press.

Shapiro, E.R. (1978). The psychodynamics and developmental psychology of the borderline patient: a review of the literature. *Amer. J. Psychiat.* 135*1305–1315.*

CHAPTER 2

Fifty Years After Freud: Dora, the Rat Man, and the Wolf-Man

No one who, like me, conjures up the most evil of those half-tamed demons that inhabit the human breast, and seeks to wrestle with them, can expect to come through the struggle unscathed.
—Freud (1)

Fifty years after his death, Freud's case histories retain an enduring interest. Written in a masterful fashion that has never been surpassed in the psychodynamic literature, they form a complex tapestry of clinical data interwoven with theoretical formulations and expositions of psychotherapeutic technique. The three major clinical accounts of analyses personally conducted by Freud are vivid portrayals not only of the patients but of Freud at work. They provide a window into the consulting room of the pioneer of psychodynamic psychotherapy as he struggles with the "demons that inhabit the human breast."

Interest in the case histories has extended outside the clinical sphere. The literary critic Steven Marcus has analyzed the Dora case as a piece of writing and concluded that Freud's account is a great work of modernist literature: "an outstanding creative and imaginative performance and an intellectual and cognitive achievement of the highest order" (2). He has suggested that the content and form of the Dora case are analogous to Ibsen's plays, but with one major difference—Freud is not only the creator of the work, he is also one of the characters in the action who suffers as much as anyone.

Beyond their historical and literary importance, the case histories illustrate the evolution of Freud's psychodynamic theory and practice, and they create a striking background against which current theoretical developments and insights into the clinical psychotherapeutic situation can be contrasted. Eissler has called Freud's case histories "the pillars upon which psychoanalysis as an empirical science rests" (3, p. 395). It is the intention of this paper to reexamine three of those pillars, Dora, the Rat Man, and the Wolf-Man, in the light of modern psychodynamic thinking and to draw attention to the heuristic value of such comprehensive case reports in an age, as Peter Gay (4) has commented, that seems to have forgotten how to write them.

DORA

In October 1900, Freud wrote to Fliess, his colleague and confidant: "It has been a lively time, and I have a new patient, a girl of eighteen; the case has opened smoothly to my collection of picklocks" (S, p. 325). This patient was destined to become famous as Dora when Freud published in 1905 his "Fragment of an Analysis of a Case of Hysteria" (1), the first of his major case studies. Dora's analysis came to an end after 3 months when she abruptly broke off the treatment, an action that shook Freud but led him to his epochal recognition of the centrality of transference in all psychotherapeutic ventures.

More than any other of Freud's case histories, Dora has generated a plethora of criticism, comment, and reanalysis since its original publication. In part, this can be viewed as a consequence of Freud's expository and literary skill, which lends his account a compelling narrative thrust while simultaneously providing a wealth of clinical material concerning Dora and the unfolding of the treatment. Freud's questionable technique has stimulated considerable retrospective comment by clinicians, as has his countertransference to Dora. Social historians and feminist scholars (6, 7) have found much to interest them in the Dora case concerning aspects of male-female relations in late nineteenth-century Vienna, where hysteria in women appeared to flourish. Jennings (8) has suggested that the efflorescence of papers on Dora during the past two decades has been catalyzed by the development of more sophisticated theories of countertransference and adolescent psychology, which lead to a better understanding of why the treatment failed than the reasons provided by Freud.

Freud had successfully treated Dora's father, a well-to-do manufacturer, for syphilis when Dora was 10. Dora's father brought her to Freud for a consultation when she was 16. According to Freud (1), she was at that time "unmistakably neurotic," but she balked at his recommendation that she enter treatment. Two years later, Freud significantly noted that her father "handed her over to me for psychotherapeutic treatment." Ostensibly, the discovery of a note written by Dora threatening suicide, followed by a fainting spell after an argument with her father, led him to insist on her entering treatment with Freud despite her reluctance. As was to emerge, Dora rightly felt that her father had an ulterior motive in mandating her Treatment.

Freud noted that Dora had developed chronic psychogenic dyspnea at age 8. At 12 she developed migraine and tussis nervosa. The latter symptom persisted and was present, accompanied by recurrent aphonia, when Freud took her into treatment. Simultaneously she exhibited social withdrawal, fatigue, lack of concentration, and, in Freud's words, "chronically low spirits," a symptom picture consistent with depression.

Freud presented the case as further confirmation of his thesis, outlined in "Studies on Hysteria" (9), that the psychological determinants of hysteria lie with "a psychical trauma, a conflict of affect, and—an additional factor …—a disturbance in the sphere of sexuality." In Dora's case these determinants were to be found in the sexual entanglements in which Dora found herself involving her father and intimate friends of her parents, Herr and Frau K. Dora's father was miserable in his marriage and was embroiled in an affair with Frau K, while Herr K had made sexual advances to Dora when she was 16 during a vacation the two families spent together. Dora informed her parents of Herr K 's impropriety and they confronted Herr K, but he denied the episode and ascribed it to a fantasy arising out of Dora's preoccupation with sexual matters, something he had been apprised of by his wife. Dora's father confided in Freud that he agreed with Herr K that Dora was in the grip of an irrational fantasy, denied that he was having an affair with Frau K, and asserted that there was nothing to his daughter's allegations.

Freud, ever the shrewd skeptic, did not swallow Dora's father's protestations of innocence. He uncovered an earlier episode of attempted seduction of Dora by Herr K when she was 14. Dora was convinced that "she had been handed over to Herr K as the price of his tolerating the relations between her father and his wife" (1), thus justifying her rage at her father. Freud, however, observed that for some years before Herr K's attempt to kiss her when she was 16, Dora had actively colluded in facilitating the affair between her father and Frau K. Freud concluded that Dora had actually been in love with Herr K during that time and suggested that her fury at her father for his affair was fueled by her oedipal feelings, which had been aroused to defend her against conflict created by the intensity of her feelings for Herr K. Freud interpreted that Dora wanted Herr K to continue his entreaties and marry her and that she was horrified by his denial of the kissing episode at age 16 and his slandering her, thus fueling her fury at unfaithful men. Freud further elucidated that Dora and Frau K had been on the most intimate terms, had shared a bedroom together, and that unconsciously Dora had been in love with Frau K. Again, she had been betrayed when Frau K calumniated her to Dora's father and revealed their discussion of sexual topics.

The convoluted aspects of who was sexually involved with whom in this case are astonishing, indeed, and Marcus has a point in his statement that "in some sense everyone was conspiring to conceal what was going on; and in some yet further sense everyone was conspiring to deny that anything was going on at all. What we have here, on one of its sides, is a classical Victorian domestic drama that is at the same time a sexual and emotional can of worms" (2). Running through the case history is a constant theme of betrayal, manifest in Dora's feeling that she was never loved for herself but was constantly used, a conviction that was to reappear in her therapeutic relationship with Freud.

In publishing the case of Dora, Freud had two didactic purposes in mind, namely, to explicate the etiology of hysteria and to demonstrate the utility of his dream theory in clinical work. Two dreams and their painstaking analysis form the centerpiece of the report. The Dora case thus looks backward to The Interpretation of Dreams (10) and, in its exploration of the origins of hysteria, forward to the "Three Essays on the Theory of Sexuality" (11). Beyond these aspects, however, Freud provided in his retrospective review of the case the first clear clinical demonstration of transference, a discovery that was destined to revolutionize psychotherapeutic technique. He acknowledged that his failure to recognize and address the transference was central to Dora's abrupt termination, although he felt that his failure to interpret Dora's homosexuality —her attraction to Frau K—was a graver technical error, a position that would not be held today.

Gill and Muslin (12) have suggested that transference and resistances are always present and should be interpreted at all stages of an analytic treatment. In their opinion, a failure to do this leads to a premature interruption, as occurred with Dora. In a detailed study of the case report

(13), they delineated the ubiquity of transference material unrecognized by Freud. An example of this can been seen in Dora's reproach against her father that she had been handed over to Herr K so that Herr K would tolerate the affair between her father and Herr K's wife. Gill and Muslin pointed out that there was a clear transference reproach concealed behind this, for Dora's father had supported her treatment with Freud for his own ulterior purposes, and hence she had also been "handed over" to Freud.

Gill and Muslin also provided evidence for Freud's intense countertransference to Dora, most notably his response to her returning of her own volition, asking for further help, 15 months after she broke off treatment. Freud wrote (1), "one glance at her face, however, was enough to tell me that she was not in earnest over her request." As Gill and Muslin pointed out, it is incredible that he could have known this from one glance at her face. That Freud felt he was a victim of Dora's underlying craving for revenge against men is clear from his transcript, but he failed to recognize his own hostility toward this rebellious patient. He stated (1), "I do not know what kind of help she wanted from me, but I promised to forgive her for having deprived me of the satisfaction of affording her a far more radical cure for her troubles." There is evidence that the name that he chose to call his patient in the report was derived from that of his sister's maidservant. When Dora announced to Freud that she would not come again and that she had decided this 2 weeks before telling him, he replied (1), "that sounds like a maidservant or governess—a fortnight's warning." Rogow (14) speculates that in calling his patient Dora after his sister's maid, Freud may have been expressing anger as well as resentment at her abrupt termination. In essence, she had behaved like a maidservant and would be called after one.

Another reason the case goes awry revolves around Freud's single-minded scientific quest with regard to the analysis of Dora's two dreams, whose understanding he felt would uncover the origins and meaning of her conversion symptoms. Erikson (15) has observed that Freud's method of working was strongly influenced by his first professional identity as a physiological researcher and that at the time, "his clinical method was conceived of as an analogy to clear and exact laboratory work." Dora again felt that she was being used for an ulterior purpose, in this case Freud's scientific explorations, just as the referral to Freud by her father was, in part, an attempt to buy her silence concerning the tortuous and convoluted secrets of who was sexually involved with whom. Even when Dora dramatically announced that she had come for her last session, Freud, apparently nonplussed, insisted on continuing, in his "scientific" way, with the analysis of her second dream, rather than immediately addressing the threat to the integrity of the treatment, as would be standard practice today.

The fact that Dora was an adolescent, with all its attendant developmental considerations, was ignored by Freud, who treated her as an "experienced," mature woman. In the course of her treatment, one sexual interpretation followed another with breathtaking speed in a manner that must have been overwhelming to Dora. Freud's "picklock" metaphor in his letter to Fliess seems apt, indeed, as libidinal interpretations were thrust upon her. Blos has commented,

As we consider Dora's disruption of her analysis in developmental terms, we could say, today, that the consolidation of her neurotic condition had been short-circuited by the fact that her analysis was being conducted as if an adult neurosis already existed. As a consequence, the adolescent ego became overwhelmed by interpretations it was unable to integrate, and it simply took to flight. If there is one thing adolescent analysis has taught us, it is that ill-timed id interpretations are unconsciously experienced by the adolescent as a parental—that is, incestuous—seduction. (16)

While Dora, with her multiple symptoms, needed individual psychotherapy, in many ways she represents a classic case of the symptom carrier for the whole family. The sexual intrigue involving her father and the K family, the disavowal by everyone around her of the sexual subterfuge to which she was subjected, and the disruption of her adolescence by her immersion in this intrigue give the case, by today's standards, indications for concurrent family therapy. Such a therapy would address the secrets and dissimulation in which Dora's father participated and help to validate her reality, something Dora spontaneously did herself when she confronted her father and Herr K after she broke off her treatment with Freud.

Given that Dora was a late adolescent, a modern therapist would be far more circumspect than Freud about making constant sexual interpretations, which inevitably provide stimuli that sexualize and inflame the transference. Recognizing that Dora did not possess a mature ego and was part of a convoluted and pathogenic reality would ensure that the therapeutic stance was far more empathic than that which Freud displayed. The follow-up by Deutsch (17), with its vitriolic and far from objective description of Dora in middle-life (he called her "one of the most repulsive hysterics" he had ever met), suggests that she had a remarkable capacity for eliciting powerful negative responses from clinicians. Today such a reaction in the therapist would be seen as part of the clinical data that would help to illuminate her psychopathology; this view would be based on the current opinion that the emotional responses of the clinician to the patient are a potential source of insight into the patient's unconscious conflicts and defenses.

Freud's response to Dora, his outrage at her for sabotaging his therapeutic quest, his desire for cure, and his refusal to further treat her when she reappeared are startling, indeed. Nonetheless, one mark of Freud's greatness was his intense interest in cases that failed, and his publication of this failed case is a testimony to his intellectual honesty and to his assertion that one gains knowledge from such cases. Such publication and subsequent reexamination hastened the progress of psychoanalysis and psychotherapy and belies Gay's wry comment that "what is astonishing about the case history of Dora is ... that he published it at all" (4, p. 255).

THE RAT MAN

Freud's treatment of Ernst Lanzer, a 29-year-old lawyer, who was to become known as the Rat Man, began in October 1907 and lasted 11 months. Freud discussed the case while it was in progress at the Vienna Psychoanalytic Society and stated during one of these meetings: "In general a human being cannot bear opposed extremes in juxtaposition, be they in his personality or in his reactions. It is this endeavor for unification that we call character. In regard to persons near to us extremely opposed emotions may be so strong as to become completely unbearable" (18, p. 263).

This comment goes straight to the heart of the case and Freud's didactic purpose in publishing it: the elucidation of the nature and meaning of obsessional symptoms. Freud published the finished report under the title "Notes Upon a Case of Obsessional Neurosis" in 1909 (19), but it is fortunate that his daily rough notes on the first 4 months of the treatment survived. They provide a unique entree into his day-to-day method of working, amplify aspects of the formal case report, and, as in the case of Dora, raise questions concerning his technique.

Lanzer consulted Freud complaining of obsessional thoughts that something might happen to his father and to a woman he loved, combined with a frightening impulse to cut his throat. From the beginning, Lanzer emphasized his sexual life, an early manifestation of the transference, as he assumed, on the basis of his fragmentary knowledge of Freud's theories, that this would interest Freud the most. Lanzer described the presence of a full-blown obsessional neurosis when he was 6 years old, which Freud viewed as the nucleus and prototype of the later disorder. Lanzer had the conviction that his parents could read his thoughts, such as his intense desire to see certain girls naked. Simultaneously he had "an uncanny feeling, as though something might happen if I thought such things, and as though I must do all sorts of things to prevent it" (19). His main fear as a child was that his father might die; this was the same fear he had when he entered treatment with Freud. At this point, to Freud's amazement, he learned that Lanzer's father had died several years previously.

In the second session Lanzer went on to describe the experience that had precipitated his consulting Freud. While he was on army maneuvers (Lanzer was in the Austrian military reserve), another officer recounted a horrible punishment used in the East. At this point, agitated, Lanzer broke off, got up from the couch, and begged Freud to spare him the recital of the details. Freud insisted that he continue. Lanzer described the punishment: "the criminal was tied up a pot was turned upside down on his buttocks … some rats were put into it … and they bored their way in" "Into his anus," Freud finished for him. It then emerged that Lanzer feared that both the woman whom he loved and his father were being subjected to this hideous torture, even though his father was long dead.

Lanzer's absence from his father's bedside when his father died had sent him into a paroxysm of guilt manifest in the conviction that he was a criminal. Freud interpreted to Lanzer that the affect was justified but that the sense of guilt belonged to an unconscious content of infantile origin, a murderous impulse toward his father. As if to mitigate the impact of this interpretation, Freud then delivered a brief didactic lecture to the patient on the psychological differences between the conscious and unconscious and concluded the session in a further supportive manner by saying [G] 'a word or two upon the good opinion I had formed of him, and thus gave him visible pleasure"; this was clearly a departure from the admonitions of abstinence that he later asserted in his papers on technique.

In his explication of the origins of Lanzer's suicidal impulses, Freud highlighted the centrality of aggression in obsessional neurosis. Unconscious rage directed at individuals who unwittingly thwarted Lanzer's wishes evoked a talion response—"kill yourself"—as punishment for this murderous passion, and it was this component of the process that passed into his consciousness. The battle between love and hate directed at the same object became represented in compulsive acts of doing and undoing on Lanzer's part.

As Freud attempted to uncover the origins of Lanzer's obsessional thoughts concerning the rat torture, memories of a childhood beating by his father surfaced. This was followed by a sudden eruption of fury directed at Freud: "he began heaping the grossest and filthiest abuse upon me and my family." Significantly, these outbursts would be followed by self-reproaches and Lanzer's leaping up from the couch and roaming about Freud's consulting room, fearing (and wishing) that Freud would give him a beating for his vile words, thus recapitulating his experience with his father. These events and associations led Freud to a solution of the rat idea. Hearing of this punishment had stimulated Lanzer's anal eroticism, and in an explanatory tour de force, Freud interwove aspects of the rat obsession with elements of Lanzer's recent and early life, with his childhood experience and fantasies, with his intense ambivalence toward his. father, and, finally, with the symbolic meanings of rats. In a compelling argument he came to the denouement that Lanzer himself "had been (as a child) just such a nasty wretch, who was apt to bite people when he was in a rage, and had been fearfully punished for doing so. He could truly be said to find a living likeness of himself in the rat." Meticulously, Freud interpreted to Lanzer the unconscious meaning of the various elements of his obsessional symptoms, and, with remarkable dispatch, "when we reached the solution that has been described above, the patient's rat delirium disappeared."

In the formal transcript of the case Freud is still intent, like the conscientious archaeologist with whom he liked to compare himself, in detailed uncovering of the underlying origins and meaning of Lanzer's bizarre symptoms. (A similar approach was central to the thrust of his work with Dora, where, for example, her psychogenic cough and aphonia were traced to a fantasy of fellatio stimulated by her contact through her clothes with Herr K's erection when he attempted to seduce her.) At this stage, it was this meticulous "uncovering" of repressed memories that Freud believed was the primary therapeutic component of analysis.

In the cases of both Dora and the Rat Man, the importance of the mother-child relationship gets short shrift. Dora's mother is dismissed in a brief paragraph, while Lanzer's mother is incidentally referred to on only a few occasions, as if she were of little import. When one turns to the original notes on the case, however, a different picture emerges. After Lanzer's initial consultation with Freud and his being informed of the terms of the treatment, Freud recorded that Lanzer said hie must consult his mother. The next day, after doing so, he came back and told Freud that he accepted them. Lanzer's mother's control over his life was further revealed by the fact that his inheritance from his father was in her hands and she doled out small amounts of money to her son at her discretion. Freud thus gives ample evidence of the importance of Lanzer's relationship with his mother in these rough notes, yet the significance of such material is not acknowledged in the formal report.

Lanzer gave expression to powerful feelings of aggression toward Freud during the treatment. At one point Freud noted, "he developed great irritation with me—he accused me of picking my nose, refused to shake hands with me, thought that a filthy swine like me needed to be taught manners and considered that the postcard I had sent him, and had signed 'cordially' was too intimate." For all this negative transference, as the sending of the postcard indicates, Freud maintained a strongly positive, even affectionate feeling toward Lanzer. On one occasion Freud noted, "He was hungry and was fed." This positive feeling of Freud's, coupled with solicitous actions such as literally feeding his patient, leads one to speculate that this therapeutic stance had a significant influence on Lanzer's symptomatic cure.

As Zetzel (20) has noted, Freud emphasized oedipal content in his interpretations, but anal-sadistic elements in Lanzer's basic conflict abound, particularly in the case notes in which the patient's preoccupations with buttocks, feces, and fantasies of torture are ubiquitous. In addition, Zetzel drew attention to the importance of the loss of an older sister, who died when Lanzer was 4, and highlighted his identification with his mother, which, Zetzel suggested, led Lanzer to relate to his father in an unconsciously homosexual and masochistic fashion. Freud's technique in this case has received considerable criticism by later psychoanalysts, although Zetzel has defended Freud's departures from standard analytic technique as necessary for establishing a sturdy therapeutic alliance and suggested that Lanzer's identification with Freud, a father surrogate, may have been the central factor that enabled him to resolve his intrapsychic conflicts. Kanzer (21) observed that the case represents an early phase of psychoanalytic theory and technique redolent with the conspicuous intellectual indoctrination that prevailed at that time, when the importance of reliving in the transference was not yet emphasized. Kanzer felt that Freud, in supplying Lanzer with the words "into his anus," which Lanzer was unable to say while recounting the nature of the Eastern torture, was being seduced into the role not only of the cruel officer but also of the invading rats themselves. Muslin (22) has demonstrated that in this case, understanding of the use of the transference was in transition. Transference, while acknowledged, as it was not with Dora, was of importance in establishing conviction of the validity of repressed memories. The curative aspects of the unfolding and resolution of the transference neurosis, the sine qua non of modern-day psychoanalysis and insight-oriented psychotherapy, were not yet recognized.

Lipton (23) has taken issue with those who have suggested that Freud's technique with Lanzer was only a precursor of his later "classical" technique. He marshaled evidence to show that Freud's technique did not change after the analysis of Lanzer, and the later conduct of the Wolf-Man case would tend to confirm this thesis. The question of Freud's relationship with the patient and its existing outside formal technique is at issue. Lipton argued that modern technique, with its emphasis on neutrality, has been expanded to cover the personal relationship that develops between patient and therapist but that there are dangers inherent in this, namely, that the systematic attempt to obliterate any personal influence may hinder the development of an object relationship. In Lipton's. view Freud's technique existed separate from the personal relationship between him and Lanzer, and his recognition of their separateness fostered the establishment of an object relationship that enhanced the course of the analysis.

Tragically, Lanzer died in World War I, so that long-term clinical follow-up is lacking, although Freud noted in a letter to Jung in 1909 that Lanzer had announced his engagement and was "facing life with courage and ability" (24, pp. 157, 158). Theoretical developments since Freud, particularly those exemplified by the object relations school, would lead to the contention that the impressive therapeutic effects that were obtained resulted as much from Lanzer's positive object relationship with Freud and its internalization as from interpretive work alone. The case of the Rat Man and its remarkable therapeutic results highlight the question of the nature of therapeutic action, an issue that remains controversial in dynamic psychotherapy and psychoanalysis to this day.

THE WOLF-MAN

The case history of the Wolf-Man, as Strachey has noted (25), is the most elaborate and, in Freud's eyes, the most important of his clinical accounts. Still rankled by the defections of Jung and Adler and their criticisms and dilution of his view of the crucial importance of infantile sexuality in normal development and psychopathology, Freud published "From the History of an Infantile Neurosis" (26) in 1918 with the frank polemical intent of refuting their claims and providing convincing proof of his own. The availability of accounts of the subsequent treatment of the Wolf-Man after his analysis with Freud, together with the patient's autobiography, adds a further dimension to our understanding of this patient.

By the time Sergei Pankejeff, a wealthy Russian aristocrat, came to Freud for treatment in 1910 at the age of 23, he had become a psychological invalid crippled by multiple phobias and anxieties and was unable even to dress himself. He had already consulted some of the leading psychiatrists of the day, including Emil Kraepelin, seeking relief from his condition but to no avail. His treatment lasted 4 years, at which point Freud regarded the case as completed, although subsequent events were to show that this was overly optimistic. Ernest Jones (18) has revealed that Pankejeff initiated the first hour with the offer to have rectal intercourse with Freud and then to defecate on his head! Such a beginning would give the modern psychotherapist pause, to say the least, and raise immediate questions concerning the gravity of the patient's psychopathology and psychoanalysis as the treatment of choice.

Freud began his account by noting that Pankejeff developed an animal phobia immediately before. his fourth birthday and that this was followed by an obsessional neurosis that lasted into his tenth year. This infantile neurosis, analyzed some 15 years later, is the main subject of Freud's communication. He acknowledged that his abstaining from writing a complete account of Pankejeff's adult illness, treatment, and recovery, on the grounds that such a task was technically impractical and would breach confidentiality, prevented him from demonstrating the connection between the childhood condition and the adult illness; however, he leaves no doubt in the reader's mind of his conviction that this connection is essential to an understanding of the adult condition.

Pankejeff was the younger child, born on Christmas Day, of a wealthy landowning Russian family. At the age of three and one-half, a sudden transformation occurred in his character. Formerly good-natured and agreeable, he suddenly became "discontented, unstable and violent, took offense on every possible occasion, and then flew into a rage" (26). Shortly thereafter he became terrified of a picture of a wolf in a book, which his older sister proceeded to use to torment him. Other fears of insects and horses emerged, although he recalled that simultaneously he liked to torture beetles, cut caterpillars into pieces, and beat horses. At the age of 8, he developed an obsessional neurosis, marked by religious content, that involved an identification with Christ, with whom he shared his birthday.

Freud elicited from his patient childhood memories of sexual seduction by his sister and a threat of castration from his nursemaid in response to masturbatory exhibitionism. Freud saw this arousal of castration anxiety as leading to a regression to a pregenital anal-sadistic organization that manifested itself in his childhood predilection for torturing insects and animals. Freud postulated that Pankejeff's seduction by his sister had forced him into a passive role and given him a passive sexual aim, particularly toward his father. His outbursts of rage thus had a masochistic intent, designed to elicit beatings from his father.

The *piéce de résistance* of Freud's account is his analysis of Pankejeff's anxiety dream of childhood in which he saw six or seven wolves sitting on a tree outside his bedroom window, a scene that terrified him and woke him up. This dream was to provide the case with its informal title and the pseudonym that was adopted by the patient in his autobiography. (Later in life, when Pankejeff had settled into the role of being Freud's most famous patient, he would paint pictures of this dream and give them to visiting psychoanalysts.) With his typical expository skill, Freud argued that the dream represented the child's transformation of being a witness to his parents' sexual intercourse. The pathogenic effect of this primal scene and the repudiation of his wish for sexual satisfaction from his father, with its implication of castration, resulted in the appearance of the wolf phobia. Freud concluded that this primal scene experience took place during Pankejeff's infancy, and he marshaled his considerable persuasive skills to convince the skeptical reader of this reconstruction. However, the reality of this event, as opposed to a later primal scene fantasy, remains controversial.

In analyzing the childhood obsessional neurosis, Freud delineated three sexual trends directed by Pankejeff toward his father: "from the time of the dream onwards, in his unconscious he was homosexual, and in his neurosis he was at the level of cannibalism; while the earlier masochistic attitude remained the dominant one." The cannibalistic or oral phase of libido delineated by Freud was to play a central role in his later theories of incorporation, identification, and the origins of depression. Pankejeff's religious preoccupations, doubts, fears, and ambivalence were seen as being unconsciously directed toward his father. Freud viewed Pankejeff's lack of interest in the world at large during his analysis as a consequence of his repression of his overpowerful homosexuality; however, given the family history of affective illness (both Pankejeff's father and sister committed suicide), one wonders if he was not suffering from a concomitant depressive illness.

One of Pankejeff's multitude of complaints was of a severe, intractable constipation. Freud observed how doubt is the obsessional patient's "strongest weapon, the favorite expedient of his resistance." This doubt had served to keep Pankejeff's response to the treatment negligible in terms of therapeutic results. Freud seized on the intestinal symptom as representing "the small trait of hysteria which is regularly to be found at the root of an obsessional neurosis." He promised him a return to normal bowel activity. In the face of Pankejeff's incredulity, Freud then had "the satisfaction of seeing his doubt dwindle away, as in the course of the work his bowel began, like a hysterically affected organ, to 'join in the conversation,' and in a few weeks' time recovered its normal function." Freud had spent some time analyzing Pankejeff's anal eroticism and its relationship to his feminine identification and castration anxiety and postulated that the regular enemas he received for his constipation had the symbolic meaning of copulation. Freud believed that this interpretive work resulted in the disappearance of the symptom, but the frank suggestive element in his asserting to Pankejeff that the symptom would disappear is apparent.

In Freud's view, Pankejeff's breakdown had been precipitated by his contracting gonorrhea, which caried the unconscious meaning of castration. In his infantile neurosis, the wolf phobia had broken out when e was faced with the reality that such a thing as castration was possible. It was through the unveiling of the primal scene, the uncovering of his identification with his mother, and the wish to be sexually satisfied by his father and to present him with an anal child that Freud believed the case to be resolved. The focus was thus upon the negative oedipus complex. More primitive preoedipal conflicts, particularly those involving separation, were seen as less important, and, as in the cases of Dora and the Rat Man, the mother-child relationship remained in the background.

In his introductory remarks, Freud reveals that there was no movement in this case until he set a specific termination date and hence a specific time limit on the treatment. This radical (and coercive) technical maneuver resulted in the appearance of all the material that Freud recounted concerning the infantile neurosis and allowed the treatment to advance to the point where Pankejeff's symptoms temporarily remitted. Meissner (27) has suggested that the breakthrough of resistances and flood of material that appeared as a consequence of this maneuver represented just another level of compliant submission by Pankejeff to Freud's insistence.

Offenkrantz and Tobin (28) have observed that Pankejeff was of particular interest to Freud because of his unique role in the development of the theory of infantile sexuality. Freud thus had a research interest in

Pankejeff that made him more than just another patient. In support of this, Jones (18) has noted that when Pankejeff returned for a brief period of treatment in 1919 after the Russian revolution had swept away his fortune, Freud treated him without fee and collected money to sustain him and his wife for some 6 years. Offenkrantz and Tobin raised the possibility that the day residue for the six wolves in the manifest content of the wolf dream at the time it was first reported was a photograph in Freud's consulting room of the six psychoanalysts who were his early colleagues. In this regard, they observed that the transference implications of the dream are absent from Freud's report. They postulated that Pankejeff was extremely interested in and sensitive to the two roles that Freud was playing simultaneously, both therapist and investigator. In a further study of the problems of conducting an analysis with simultaneous therapeutic and research goals (29), they suggested that such a dual function stimulates primal scene fantasies.

Freud's second treatment of Pankejeff in 1919 lasted 4 months and dealt successfully with "a piece of transference which had not hitherto been overcome," whose nature is not elaborated on by Freud (26). In 1926, Pankejeff again consulted Freud and was referred on this occasion to one of Freud's pupils, Ruth Mack Brunswick, who subsequently published an account of her 5-month treatment (30). Significantly, Brunswick's therapy was conducted without fee, which must have further confirmed Pankejeff's view of himself as a special patient.

When he came to Brunswick, Pankejeff had decompensated alarmingly and had developed a delusional paranoid psychosis with hypochondriacal features. He was convinced that he possessed a gaping hole in his nose as a consequence of the treatment of an obstructed nasal sebaceous gland by electrolysis. He was obsessed with this and felt unable to go on living in what he viewed as his irreparably mutilated state. He had formed a delusional hatred toward the physician who had treated him, although it soon became apparent that this was a substitute for Freud, whom he blamed for the loss of his fortune in Russia. Simultaneously, Pankejeff maintained (not without cause) that he had a special, favored relationship with Freud.

Brunswick attacked Pankejeff's view of himself as Freud's favorite son, which today we would view as an assault on the patient's narcissistic defenses. It emerged that Pankejeff's decompensation had been precipitated by his learning of Freud's life-threatening illness, the cancer of the palate that was ultimately to prove fatal. Meissner (27), reviewing the case from the perspective of Kohut's self psychology, postulated that Freud had served as an idealized self-object with whom Pankejeff had developed an idealizing narcissistic transference and that his psychological equilibrium was gravely threatened by Freud's illness.

Brunswick focused on interpreting Pankejeff's castration anxiety and death wishes toward his father and Freud. In the midst of this Pankejeff became more floridly psychotic: "He talked wildly in terms of his fantasies, completely cut off from reality. He threatened to shoot both Freud and me … and somehow these threats sounded less empty than those which one is accustomed to hear" (30). Following a dream in which Brunswick appeared as his mother, who destroys religion and frees him from his identification with the suffering Christ, Pankejeff's psychotic state remitted with surprising rapidity. Meissner (27) suggested that this rapid recovery was a consequence of the formation of a new narcissistic object relationship with Brunswick, accompanied by fantasies of protective omnipotence to replace the threatened loss of the idealized self-object, whom Freud represented.

From the vantage point of present-day nosology it seems that Pankejeff suffered from a severe borderline disorder with narcissistic features. His outrageous opening suggestions to Freud, his intense and unresolved narcissistic transference, and his transient psychotic decompensation all tend to support this diagnosis. His grandiose narcissism was sustained in later years by his view of himself as the most famous psychoanalytic case (or as the Wolf-Man remembered Freud's words, "a piece of psychoanalysis"

[27)), and he suffered no further psychotic relapses. This has to be viewed as a reasonable outcome given the degree of pathology but one that was a consequence of a therapeutic process very different from that posited by Freud or Brunswick.

DISCUSSION

While it is apparent to the reader of these three case histories that Freud was as much a protagonist in each unfolding clinical drama as the patients themselves, his primary focus remained their intrapsychic context and not their interaction with him. One of the more important developments in psychodynamic theory and technique since Freud's time involves the recognition that a two-person psychology is at work in the clinical situation. As Balint (31) has observed, "our theory and technique refer to events occurring between two people and not simply within one person." The interaction between Freud and his patients, the new object relationship that was formed in the therapeutic setting, is of far greater import than he recognized. For Freud, interpretation was the curative agent, but Loewald (32) has suggested that therapeutic effects are a consequence of ego development resuming in therapy as a result of the relationship with a new object. Loewald drew a parallel between the use of object relations in the formation and development of the psychic apparatus during childhood and the dynamics of the therapeutic process. In his view, the ego development that may take place in therapy is not simply the internalization of objects but an internalization of an interaction process between patient and therapist that includes, but is not confined to, interpretive work. Therapeutic action may thus be viewed as a resumption of growth and the completion of development.

An argument can be made that this process was very much at work in the cases of the Rat Man and the Wolf-Man. Therapeutic effects in Freud's view resulted from the interpretation and working through of instinctual urges, resistances, and transference, whereby what was unconscious became conscious. Cooper (33) has drawn attention to the radical departure from this model represented by Loewald's conception of the interactive role of the therapist, with its emphasis on empathic communication and the therapeutic relationship. He noted that Kohut, shorn of his special metapsychology, is also very close to sharing this outlook. Freud was not unaware of the importance of the therapeutic relationship as a mutative factor in treatment. In one of his last papers (34) he stated that the positive transference "is the strongest motive for the patient's taking a share in the joint work"; however, he did not develop the theoretical implications of the therapeutic relationship and, specifically, of supportive measures in therapy, although, as is clear from the Rat Man and the Wolf-Man cases, he empirically used them.

Similarly, the increasing awareness since Freud's time of the crucial importance of the mother-child relationship in development has led clinicians such as Winnicott (35) to view the psychotherapeutic setting as containing a revival of elements of that relationship. This developmental perspective and its corollary, the importance of preoedipal conflict and dynamics, are generally absent from Freud's case histories, where the emphasis is much more upon the relationship with the father; however, manifestations of preoedipal elements can be seen in his case reports. Mahler's work on selfobject differentiation and separation-individuation in the child's preoedipal phase (36) has had a profound influence on modern theories of therapy and practice. Modell (37) has emphasized the relevance of developmental concepts such as the holding environment to the therapeutic situation and the dual function of transference as both a recapitulation of early developmental conflicts and a transference neurosis. These perspectives allow a broader view on the nature of psychodynamic therapy than existed in Freud's time and provide a framework for the psychotherapeutic treatment of the more disturbed patient such as the Wolf-Man.

In his papers on technique (38–42), Freud promulgated clear guidelines and a compelling clinical rationale for preserving therapeutic neutrality. He stated, "As far as his relations with the physician are concerned, the patient must be left with unfulfilled wishes in abundance. It is expedient to deny him precisely those satisfactions which he desires most intensely and expresses most importunately" (42). At first glance, it would appear that Freud abrogated his own maxims in his treatments of the Rat Man and the Wolf-Man. A closer examination of his "extra-analytic" behavior with these two patients, however, draws attention to a complex issue concerning what Stone (43) has called the "real personal relationship" between therapist and patient versus the "true transference reactions." The impact of personal interactions between the therapist and the patient has been a neglected subject in the literature, perhaps because of the uneasy feelings that are stirred up in clinicians who fear that the "purity" of the therapeutic field is compromised by such occurrences. That such personal interactions in the therapeutic encounter are inevitable, however, can hardly be disputed, and Anna Freud has commented,

> But—so far as the patient has a healthy part of his personality, his real relationship to the analyst is never wholly submerged. With due respect for the necessary strictest handling and interpretation of the transference, I still feel that we should leave room somewhere for the realization that analyst and patient are also two real people, of equal adult status, in a real personal relationship to each other. I wonder whether our—at times complete—neglect of this side of the matter is not responsible for some of the hostile reactions which we get from our patients and which we are apt to ascribe to "true transference" only. (44)

Greenson and Wexler (45) have asserted that it is essential to acknowledge, differentiate, and even nurture the nontransference or relatively transference-free reactions between patient and therapist in order to facilitate the full flowering and ultimate resolution of the patient's transference. It could be said that Freud did not necessarily breach analytic neutrality in the clinical setting where the transference was involved but that his personal warmth and regard for both the Rat Man and the Wolf-Man, manifest in his extra-analytic actions, fostered the recognition of that "equal adult status" and "real personal relationship" which are intrinsic to the clinical situation and thus enhanced the therapeutic process.

The continuous commentary that the case histories have evoked since their publication speaks to their intellectually provocative quality and the degree to which they can involve the reader. Mahony (46) has asserted that the sometimes fragmentary nature of the clinical material provided by Freud invites the reader to participate and engage in a synthetic process of his or her own. There seems little danger of Freud's case histories becoming mere historical curiosities. Like all truly creative works, they continuously pose new meanings and questions. It can be argued that, as examples of clinical exposition and persuasion, they will never be surpassed. Such a status, however, rather than discouraging the writing of new comprehensive case reports, should foster their appearance. The heuristic value of such comprehensive psychodynamic case reporting is considerable, and the progress of dynamic psychotherapy and the level of scientific discourse concerning its theory and technique would only be enhanced by resurrecting the tradition begun by Freud.

REFERENCES

1. Freud S: Fragment of an analysis of a case of hysteria (1905 (1901]), *Standard Edition,* vol 7, 1953.

2. Marcus S: (1987). Freud and Dora: story, history, case history, in *Freud and the Culture of Psychoanalysis.* New York, WW Norton.

3. Eissler KR: (1965). *Medical Orthodoxy and the Future of Psychoanalysis.* New York, International Universities Press.

4. Gay P: *Freud: A Life for Our Time.* New York, Norton.

5. Freud S: (1954).*The Origins of Psychoanalysis: Letters to Wilhelm Fliess, Drafts and Notes, 1887–1902.* Edited by Bonaparte M, Freud A, Kris E. New York, Basic Books.

6. Decker H: (1981). Freud and Dora: constraints on medical progress. *Soc Hist* 14(3):445-64.

7. Bernheimer C, Kahane C (eds) (1987). In *Dora's Case: Freud, Hysteria, Feminism.* New York, Columbia University Press.

8. Jennings JL: (1986). The revival of Dora. *J A. Psychoanal Assoc;* 34:607–635.

9. Breuer J, Freud S: (1895[1893–1895]), Studies I on hysteria *Standard Edition* vol 2.

10. Freud S: (1900). The Interpretation of Dreams *Standard Edition* vols 4–5.

11. Freud S: (1905). Three essays on the theory of sexuality *Standard Edition,* vol 7.

12. Gill MM, Muslin HL: (1976). Early interpretation of transference. *J Am Psychoanal Assoc* 24779–794.

13. Muslin HL, Gill MM:(1978). Transference in the Dora case. *J Am Psychoanal Assoc* 26:311–328.

14. Rogow AA: (1978). A further footnote to Freud's "Fragment of a case of hysteria." *J Am Psychoanal Assoc* 26:330–356.

15. 1Erikson EH: (1962). Reality and actuality. *J Am Psychoanal Assoc.* 10:451-474.

16. Blos P: (1972). The epigenesis of the adult neurosis. *Psychoanal Study Child*; 27:106-135

17. Deutsch F: (1957). A footnote to Freud's "Fragment of a case of hysteria." *Psychoanal Q*; 26: 159–167.

18. Jones E: (1955). *Sigmund Freud Life and Work, Volume Two: Years of Maturity 1901-1919* 46:i-xx.

19. Freud S: (1955). Notes upon a case of obsessional neurosis (1909), in *Standard Edition*, vol 10.

20. Zetzel E (1970.), An obsessional neurotic; Freud's Rat Man, *in The Capacity for Emotional Growth.* New York, International Universities Press

21. Kanzer M: (1952). The transference neurosis of the Rat Man. *Psychoanal Q* 212181-189

22. Muslin H.L. (1979). Transference in the Rat Man case: the transference in transition. *J Am Psychoanal Assoc* 27:561–578.

23. Lipton S.D. (1977). The advantages of Freud's technique as shown in his analysis of the Rat Man. *Int J Psychoanal*; 58:255–273.

24. McGuire W (ed): (1974). *The Freud/Jung Letters: The Correspondence Between Sigmund Freud and CG Jung.* Translated by Mannheim R, Hull RFC. Princeton, NJ, Princeton University Press.

25. Strachey J: (1955). editor's note to "From the history of an infantile neurosis." *Standard Edition*, vol 17..

26. Freud S: From the history of an infantile neurosis (1918 [1914]). Ibid, vol 17, 1955.

27. Meissner WW: The Wolf-Man and the paranoid process. *Annual of Psychoanalysis* 1977; 5:27–74.

28. Offenkrantz W, Tobin A: (1973). Problems of the therapeutic alliance: Freud and the Wolf-Man. *Int J Psychoanal* 54: 75–78.

29. Offenkrantz W, Tobin A: (1978). Problems of the therapeutic alliance: analysis with simultaneous therapeutic and research goals. *Int Rev Psychoanal* 5:217–230.

30. Brunswick R.M. (1971). A supplement to Freud's "History of an infantile neurosis," in *The Wolf-Man by the Wolf-Man*. Edited by Gardiner M. New York, Basic Books.

31. Balint M: (1950), Changing therapeutic aims and techniques in psychoanalysis. *Int J Psychoanal* 31: 117–124.

32. Loewald H.W. (1980). On the therapeutic action of psychoanalysis, in *Papers on Psychoanalysis*. New Haven, Yale University Press

33. Cooper A.M. (1988). Our changing views of the therapeutic action of psychoanalysis. Psychoanal Q; 57: 15–27.

34. Freud S; (1964). Analysis terminable and interminable (1937), *Standard Edition,* vol 23.

35. Winnicott D.W. (1958). *Collected Papers: Through Paediatrics To Psycho-Analysis.* London, Tavistock Publications.

36. Mahler M: (1967). On human symbiosis and the vicissitudes of individuation. *J Am Psychoanal Assoc*; IS: 740–763.

37. Modell A.M. (1984). *Psychoanalysis in a New Context.* New York, international Universities Press,

38. Freud S: (1912). The dynamics of transference *Standard Edition,* vol 12. 1958

39. Freud S: (1912). Recommendations to physicians practicing psychoanalysis *Standard Edition,* vol 12, 1958.

40. Freud S: (1913). On beginning the treatment: further recommendations on the technique of psycho-analysis, ! *Standard Edition* vol 12, 1958.

41. Freud S: (1915 [1914]). Observations on transference-love: further recommendations on the technique of psycho-analysis, III *Standard Edition* vol 12, 1958.

42. Freud S: Lines of advance in psycho-analytic therapy (1919 [1918]). *Standard Edition* vol 17, 1955.
43. Stone L: (1961). *The Psychoanalytic Situation*. New York, International Universities Press.:
44. Freud A, (1954). The widening scope of indications for psychoanalysis: discussion. *J Am Psychoanal Assoc vol 2, 607–620.*.
45. Greenson R.R. & Wexler M (1969). The non-transference relationship in the psychoanalytic situation. *Int J Psychoanal* 50:27–39.
46. Mahony P.H. (1984).*Cries of the Wolf-Man*. New York, International Universities Press,

CHAPTER 3

Mystical Experience and Psychosis

It has often been noted clinically that the onset of an acute psychotic episode may be heralded by a state of confusion and acute anxiety which is then replaced by the psychotic individual's sudden "understanding" of the "meaning" of the experience. This "understanding" may include the belief that the person has been chosen to be God's agent, if not the Messiah, and a conviction that knowledge hidden from others is now in his or her grasp. This sense of noesis is often accompanied by a state of exultation and a feeling of being in direct communion with God.

A representative account of such an episode is to be found in Morag Coate's (1965) description of the onset of her psychosis:

> I got up from where I had been sitting and moved into another room. Suddenly my whole being was filled with light and loveliness and with an upsurge of deeply moving feeling from within myself to meet and reciprocate the influence that flowed into me. I was in a state of the most vivid awareness and illumination. What can I say of it? A cloudless, cerulean blue sky of the mind, shot through with shafts of exquisite, warm, dazzling sunlight. In its first and most intense stage it lasted perhaps half an hour. It seemed that some force or impulse from without were acting on me, looking into me; that I was in touch with a reality beyond my own; that I had made direct contact with the secret, ultimate source of life. What I had

read of the accounts of others acquired suddenly a new meaning. It flashed across my mind, "This is what the mystics mean by the direct experience of God."

While studying the mystical experiences that occurred to some members of a contemporary religious cult (Buckley and Galanter 1979), I was struck by the similarities between the accounts of nonpsychotic members of the sect who had undergone acute mystical episodes and subjective accounts of experiences of "significance" in psychosis. Just as in some cases of acute psychosis, a period of confusion and anxiety would be replaced by a revelation.

One member of the sect described his mystical experience thus:

I was desperately lonely and anxious a lot of the time, completely unsure as to what I wanted to do with myself. I was really depressed. Then I attended Satsang [The term for a polemical sermon in this particular cult]. I liked the way everybody there seemed to belong, and I really liked the fact that they believed in something. The second time I went I had this amazing experience. The woman giving Satsang suddenly seemed to be surrounded by light, like a glowing halo. This golden light filled the room and gradually extended to fill my whole self so that was filled with this light. I felt uplifted, happier than I could remember being. I knew then that I was in the presence of God. Time seemed to stand still. I knew with absolute conviction that Satsang was the truth. From that time on my depression vanished [p. 283].

The similarity between some aspects of mystical experience and the onset of psychosis has been noted previously by clinical researchers such as Bowers and Freedman (1966). They reported subjective accounts by patients of "psychedelic" experiences in some early psychotic reactions, and compared these to the phenomena seen in certain natural and drug-induced states. They noted that all these states have an experiential characteristic in common, of heightened consciousness or awareness.

Recently there has been an increase in interest in studying auto-biographical accounts of psychosis. Freedman (1974) has suggested that a careful examination of these accounts could generate a number of hypotheses about schizophrenic cognition and perception and be potentially useful in differentiating subtypes of the schizophrenic syndrome.

A systematic comparison of the subjective phenomenology of hallucinogen-ingestion and schizophrenia as derived from autobiographical accounts was presented by Kleinman, Gillin, and Wyatt (1977). They concluded that there was not a very good correspondence between the two states, but they did note that many of the phenomena experienced by schizophrenics have been reported by users of hallucinogens.

I felt that a similar comparison between autobiographical accounts of mystical experiences and schizophrenia would be of interest in light of the similarities that have been observed between some religious-conversion experiences and acute psychotic episodes.

FIRST-PERSON ACCOUNTS OF MYSTICAL EXPERIENCES

The classical mystical experience has usually been interpreted by those who have undergone it as a union with the divine, a union which is considered the ultimate reality and hence transcendental in nature. Though mystics have frequently stated that the experience is ineffable, their descriptions spanning a vast gulf of time and religion are remarkably consistent.

One of the earliest extant accounts of a mystical experience is to be found in St. Augustine's (1943) *Confessions:*

Our conversation had brought us to this point that any pleasure whatsoever of the bodily senses, in any brightness whatsoever of corporeal light, seemed to us not worthy of comparison with the pleasure of that eternal Light, not worthy even of mention. Rising as our love flamed upward to that Selfsame, we passed in review the various levels of bodily things, up to the heavens themselves whence sun and moon and stars shine upon this earth. And higher still we soared, thinking in our minds and speaking and marveling at Your works: and so we came to our own souls, and went beyond them to come at last to the region of richness unending, where You feed Israel forever with the food of Truth: and there life is that Wisdom by which all things are made, both the things that have been and the things that are yet to be. But this Wisdom itself is not made it is as it has ever been, and so it shall be forever: indeed "has ever been" and "shall be forever" have no place in it, but it simply is, for it is eternal [p. 164].

This description of St. Augustine's may be compared with John Custance's (1952) description of his psychosis:

From the first, the experience seemed to me to be holy. What was was the Power of Love—the name came to me at once—the Power that I knew somehow to have made all universes, past, present and to come, to be utterly infinite, and infinity of infinities, to have conquered the Power of Hate, its opposite, and thus created the sun, the stars, the moon, the planets, the earth, light, life, joy and peace, never-ending....

In that peace I felt utterly and completely forgiven, relieved from all burden of sin. The whole infinity seemed to open up before me, and during the weeks and months which followed I passed through experiences which are virtually indescribable. The complete transformation of "reality" transported me as if it were into the Kingdom of Heaven. The ordinary beauties of nature, particularly, I remember, the skies at sunrise and sunset took on a transcendental loveliness beyond belief. Every morning, quite contrary to my usual sluggish habits, I jumped up to look at them, and when possible went out to drink in, in a sort of ecstasy, the freshness of the morning air.

I feel so close to God, so inspired by His Spirit that in a sense I am God. I see the future, plan the Universe, save mankind; I am utterly and completely immortal; I am even male and female. The whole Universe, animate and inanimate, past, present, and future is with In me. All nature and life, all spirits, are co-operating and connected with me; all things are possible [pp. 46, 51].

In both accounts, the feeling of being transported beyond the self to a new realm, together with the effect of ecstasy and a heightened state of awareness, is common.

Loss of self-object boundaries, a frequent accompaniment of acute psychosis, is often seen in the classic mystic experience of which the following account is representative:

It was as if I had never realized how lovely the world was. I lay down on my back in the warm, dry moss and listened to the skylark singing as it mounted up from the fields near the sea into the dark clear sky. No other music gave me the same pleasure as that passionately joyous singing. It was a kind of leaping, exultant ecstasy, a bright, flamelike sound, rejoicing in itself. And then a curious experience befell me. It was as if everything that had seemed to be external and around me were suddenly within me. The whole world seemed to be within me. It was within me that the trees waved

59

their green branches, it was within me that the skylark was singing, it was within me that the hot sun shone, and that the shade was cool. A cloud rose in the sky, and passed in a light shower that pattered on the leaves, and I felt its freshness dropping into my soul, and I felt in all my being the delicious fragrance of the earth and the grass and the plants and the rich brown soil. I could have sobbed for joy. [Reid 1902 p. 42].

Distortion of time-sense, in particular time-dilation, is also often described in the mystic experience:

Rapt in Beethoven's music, I closed my eyes and watched a silver glow which shaped itself into a circle with a central focus brighter than the rest.... Swiftly and smoothly, I was borne through the tunnel.... The light grew brighter.... I came to a point where time and motion ceased [Allen, cited in Happold 1963, p. 133].

Schreber (1955), in his classic autobiography of his psychosis, recounted the experience of time standing still:

From the sum total of my recollections, the impression gained hold of me that the period in question, which, according to human calculation, stretched over only three to four months, had covered an immensely long period; it was as if single nights had the duration of centuries, so that within that time the most profound alterations in the whole of mankind, in the earth itself and the whole solar system could very well have taken place [p. 84].

Frank perceptual changes are common to the psychotic state and the mystical experience. These changes include synesthesia, and either the dampening of or the heightening of perceptions. Custance (1952), in describing his psychosis, wrote:

> First and foremost, comes a genera) sense of intense well-being—
> the pleasurable and sometimes ecstatic feeling tone remains as a
> sort of permanent background—closely allied with this permanent
> background is—the "heightened sense of reality." If I am to judge
> by my own experience this "heightened sense of reality" consists
> of a considerable number of related sensations, the net result of
> which is that the outer world makes a much more vivid and intense
> impression on me than usual—The first thing I note is the peculiar
> appearances of the lights—they are not exactly brighter, but deeper,
> more intense, perhaps a trifle more ruddy than usual. Certainly
> my sense of touch is heightened—my hearing appears to be more
> sensitive, and I am able to take in without disturbance or distraction
> many different sound impressions at the same time—It is actually a
> sense of communion in the first place with God, and in the second
> place with all mankind, indeed with all creation—the sense of
> communion extends to all fellow creatures with whom I come into
> contact [pp. 30–40].

Happold (1963, p. 85), in his study of mysticism, notes that in the classic mystical experience there is frequently found a new vision of the phenomenal world "as if there had been an abnormal sharpening of the senses." A member of a religious cult (Buckley & Galanter 1979) described the following experience: "Everything in the room became clearer—colors were brighter, much more intense, glowing almost. I felt as if I was in eternity."

Frank hallucinations also may be found in the mystical experience. These are more often of visual than auditory type. St. Teresa of Avila (quoted in Underhill 1961) wrote:

It was our Lord's will that in this vision I should see the angel in this wise. He was not large, but small in stature. and most beautiful—his face burning, as if he were one of the highest angels, who seem to be all on fire.... I saw in his hand a long spear of gold, and at the iron's point there seemed to be a little fire. He appeared to me to be thrusting it at times into my heart, and to pierce my very entrails; when he drew it out, he seemed to draw them out also and to leave me all on fire with a great love of God [p. 292].

The sensation of seeing and being enveloped in "light" may be common to both states. The founder of Alcoholics Anonymous (1957) described his conversion in the following manner:

My depression deepened unbearably, and finally it seemed to me as if I were at the very bottom of the pit. I still gagged badly on the notion of a Power greater than myself, but finally, just for the moment, the last vestige of my proud obstinacy was crushed. All at once, I found myself crying out, "If there is a God, let Him show Himself! I am ready to do anything, anything!"

Suddenly the room lit up with a great white light. I was caught up into an ecstasy which there are no words to describe. It seemed to me, in the mind's eye, that I was on a mountain and that a wind not of air but of spirit was blowing. And then it burst upon me that I was a free man. Slowly the ecstasy subsided, I lay on the bed, but now for a time I was in another world, a new world of consciousness. All about me there was a wonderful feeling of Presence, and I thought to myself, "So this is the God of the preachers." A great peace stole over me, and I thought, "No matter how wrong things seem to be, they are still right. Things are all right with God and His world" [p. 63].

Coate (1965) described the following during one of her psychotic episodes:

> I went back into my own room and got into bed, but now I could not sleep, and this was dangerous for the room was filled with an unearthly light and my hand cast no shadow on the wall…. Time was stretched out like an elastic hand, each minute of it was at once thinner and longer than usual. At last, the stage was reached when external time ceased altogether and only I lived on. [p. 58].

POSSESSION CULTS AND MYSTICAL UNION

Lewis (1971), in his study of ecstatic religion, has shown how ubiquitous the "seizure of man by divinity" has been in the religions of many disparate cultures. Such transcendental experiences have usually been conceived of as states of "possession" by God.

As Sargant (1975) has noted, such possession states are often deliberately induced in religious cults to give the individual the most direct and immediate experience of God, by becoming his living vessel. In Euripides' *Bacchae,* a vivid description is provided of such self-induced possession states. The Bacchantes, through their frenzied dancing, enter the ecstatic state of merging with the Godhead. In the Voodoo religion of Haiti. a contemporary form of the Dionysian bacchanale, possession regularly occurs among the participants (Metraux 1959). The rhythmic drumming and dancing which accompany Voodoo ceremonies appear to facilitate the entry into such possession states.

Maya Deren (1970), a European woman who took part in Voodoo ceremonies, described one of her possession experiences in the following manner:

My skull is a drum; each great beat drives that leg, like the point of a stake, into the ground. The singing is at my very ear, inside my head. This sound will drown me! "Why don't they stop! Why don't they stop!" I cannot wrench the leg free. I am caught in this cylinder, this well of sound. There is nothing anywhere except this. There is no way out. The white darkness moves up the veins of my leg like a swift tide rising, rising; is a great force which I cannot sustain or contain, which, surely, will burst my skin. It is too much, too much, too bright, too white for me; this is its darkness. "Mercy!" I scream within me. I hear it echoed by the voices, shrill and unearthly; "Erzulie!" The bright darkness floods up through my body, reaches my head, engulfs me. I am sucked down and exploded upward at once. That is all [p. 260].

Deren goes on to describe an experience of synesthesia:

My memory begins with sound heard distantly, addressed to me, and this I know: this is the sound of light. It is heard light, a beam invisible but bright, scanning the void for substance to fix upon; and to become upon that substance light. Around the sharp directness and direction of that sound the darkness shapes itself and now it is as if I lay at the far distant end of an infinitely deep-down, sunken well. Slowly still, borne on its lightless beam, as one might rise up from the bottom of the sea, so I rise up, the body growing lighter with each sound. The thundering rattle, clangoring bell, unbearable, then suddenly: surface; suddenly: air; suddenly: sound is light, dazzling white.

How clear the world looks in this first total light. How purely form it is, without, for the moment, the shadow of meaning. I see everything, all at once, without the delays of succession, and each detail is equal and equally lucid [p. 261].

Bourguignon (1976) has noted that the cultural institutionalization of such possession states is widespread. In his worldwide sample of 488 societies, 52 percent have possession trance as a part of their indigenous religion. He concludes that in the possession trance one is dealing with a human potential that is utilized by the vast majority of societies.

EXPERIMENTALLY INDUCED MYSTICAL EXPERIENCES

By reviewing the mystic literature, Deikman (1963, 1966) observed that the procedure of contemplative meditation has been a principal agent in producing the mystic experience. He conducted an experimental study of contemplative meditation and was able to evoke a number of phenomena in some of his subjects, including heightened sensory vividness, time distortion, a feeling of merging with the object that was being concentrated on, and fusing and alteration of normal perceptual modes.

Examples given by his subjects at different sessions of their contemplative meditation included the following:

... somewhere between the matter that is the wall and myself, somewhere in between the matter is this moving, this vibrating light and motion and power and very real substance ... it's so real and so vital that I feel as though I could reach out and take a chunk off and hand it to you.

It seems as if you were turning a light down, that you were turning the intensity of the light down and I still had this kind of shimmering sensation of very bright light simultaneous with the idea that everything is getting dark.

You can't discern shimmering in the room, can you, a color or bright shimmering in this whole area....

Well, it's very real to me, it's so real that I feel you ought to be able to see it [p. 104].

The ease with which he could evoke these phenomena in his subjects suggested to Deikman that a capacity exists, under conditions of minimal stress, for an alteration in the perception of the world and the self that is far greater than is customarily assumed to be the case for normal people.

He concluded that the classical mystic experience, LSD reactions, and certain phases of acute psychosis represent conditions of special receptivity to ordinary stimuli that are ordinarily excluded or ignored in the normal state of consciousness. This is consistent with the hypothesis that a breakdown in the "stimulus barrier" is responsible for some of the subjective phenomena experienced during psychosis.

CONCLUSIONS

The subjective experience of some psychotic episodes at their onset, and of the acute mystical experience, appear from these accounts to share some characteristics. The appearance of a powerful sense of noesis, heightening of perception, feelings of communion with the "divine," and exultation may be common to both. The disruption of thought seen in the acute psychoses, however, is not a component of the accounts of acute mystical experience reviewed here. The self-limited and generally brief span of mystical experiences also differentiates them from the psychoses. This differentiation, however, in at least one possible subtype of schizophrenia—schizophreniform psychosis—is less clear cut since these psychoses may also be self-limited and resolve without psychotic sequelae such as crystallized delusions, blunted affect, or impaired social relations. Clinical observations of the self-limited nature and good prognosis of schizophreniform psychoses, together with their affect-laden presentation, have led to the hypothesis that they are in fact variants of the affective disorders (Pope & Lipinsky 1978). This raises the possibility that what is shared by some acute psychotic states and the classic mystical experience is simply an ecstatic affective change which imbues perception with an increased intensity.

Schizophrenic disorders that have a more insidious onset seem to have little in common with the acute mystical experience. Thought blocking and other disturbances in language and speech do not appear to accompany the mystical experience. Auditory hallucinations are less common than visual hallucinations, and flatness of affect is not an accompaniment or sequel of the mystical state. Other phenomena that may occur in acute psychotic states, such as self-destructive acts and aggressive and sexual outbursts, are not a part of the mystical experience, though the latter have been observed in some states of "possession."

The ease with which elements of the acute mystical experience can be induced in possession cults or even in an experimental situation suggests that the capacity for such an altered state experience may be latently present in many people. Bowers and Freedman (1966) have suggested that the wide range of contexts in which states of heightened awareness are found to occur, and the variety of initiating causes reflect an innate capacity of the human mind. This particular altered state of consciousness may form a final common pathway for the mystical experience and at least some variants of acute psychosis. To a large extent, the content will be determined by the social context and the personality and psychodynamics of the individual undergoing the experience, but certain structural phenomena such as the heightening of perception and the feeling of transcendence seem to be constant. This raises the possibility that there is a limited repertoire of response within the central nervous system for such altered-state experiences, even though the precipitants for entering this altered state may be extremely different. Though the correspondence between the comparatively benign mystical experience and the onset of acute psychosis is a limited one, sufficient overlap exists to warrant systematic biological and psychological investigation of such altered-state experiences in the hope of illuminating further the nature of both.

REFERENCES

Alcoholics Anonymous Comes of Age.(1957). New York: Alcoholics Anonymous Publishing.

Bourguignon, E. (1976). Possession and trance in cross-cultural studies of mental health. In: Lebra, W.P., ed. *Culture-Bound Syndromes, Ethnopsychiatry and Alternate Therapists.* Honolulu: The University Press of Hawaii, pp. 47–55.

Bowers, M.B., Jr., & Freedman, D.X. (1966). "Psychedelic" experiences in acute psychoses. *Archives of General Psychiatry,* 15:240–248.

Buckley, P., & Galanter, M. (1979.). Mystical experience, spiritual knowledge, and a contemporary ecstatic religion. *British Journal of Medical Psychology,* 52:281–289.

Coate, M. (1965). *Beyond All Reason.* New York: J.B. Lippincott.

Custance, J. (1952). *Wisdom, Madness, and Folly.* New York: Pellegrini and Cudahy.

Deikman, A.J. (1963). Experimental meditation. *Journal of Nervous and Mental Disease,* 136:329–343,

———— (1966). Implications of experimentally induced contemplative meditation. *Journal of Nervous and Mental Disease,* 142:101–116.

Deren, M. (1972). *Divine Horsemen: The Voodoo Gods of Haiti.* New York: Delta.

Freedman, B.J. (1963). The subjective experience of perceptual and cognitive disturbances in schizophrenia: A review of autobiographical accounts. *Archives of General Psychiatry,* 30:333–340, 1974.

Happold, F.C. (1964). *Mysticism.* Baltimore: Penguin Books.

Kleinman, J.E.; Gillin, J.C., & Wyatt, R.J. (1977). A comparison of the phenomenology of hallucinogens and schizophrenia from some autobiographical accounts. *Schizophrenia Bulletin,* 3:560–586.

Lewis, I.M. (1971). *Ecstatic religion: An anthropological study of spirit possession and shamanism.* Baltimore: Penguin Books.

Metraux, A. (1953). *Voodoo.* New York: Oxford University Press.

Pope, H.G., Jr., & Lipinski, J.F. (1978). Diagnosis in schizophrenia and manic-depressive illness. *Archives of General Psychiatry,* 35:811–828.

Reid, F. (1902). *Following Darkness.* London: Arnold.

St. Augustine. (1943). *Confessions.* Translated by F.K. Sheed. New York: Sheed and Ward.

Sargant, W. (1975). *The Mind Possessed.* Baltimore: Penguin Books.

Schreber, D.P. (1955). *Memoirs of My Nervous Illness.* London: William Dawson and Sons Ltd.

Underhill, E. (1961). *Mysticism.* New York: E.P. Dutton.

CHAPTER 4

Observing the Other: Reflections on Anthropological Fieldwork

"But the wilderness had found him out early—I think it had whispered to him things about himself which he did not know, things of which he had no conception till he took counsel with this great solitude—and the whisper had proved irresistibly fascinating."
—J. Conrad—Heart of Darkness

Fieldwork is regarded as the crucial and distinguishing experience in forming the professional identity of the cultural anthropologist. Typically, fieldwork involves the nascent anthropologist in an immersion in another culture which is observed and studied at length. The fieldworker lives among those being studied, partaking of their lives and customs, yet simultaneously standing outside as an observer. The somewhat overworked descriptive term 'participant-observer' seems particularly apt in this instance.

In its intensity, involvement and potentially transforming impact, both psychologically and professionally, upon the budding anthropologist, fieldwork plays a role analogous to that of the training analysis in the development of the psychoanalyst. It is the *sine qua non* of one's professional identity and one is never quite the same after the experience.

Kracke (1987) has stated that the experience of immersion in a culture very different from one's own constitutes the central subject matter of cultural anthropology and virtually defines its domain as a discipline.

He observes, however, that little serious discussion has taken place in the anthropological literature on the actual experience of confronting another culture. Of perhaps greater import, there is a paucity of theoretical formulation on the psychological nature of fieldwork. Given the centrality of fieldwork to cultural anthropology, the relative absence of such theoretical development is surprising and stands in striking contrast to the sister discipline of psychoanalysis where, beginning with Freud, a voluminous clinical and theoretical literature exists on the nature of the experience of conducting an analysis.

In this paper, I shall attempt to develop a psychoanalytic hypothesis concerning the psychological nature of fieldwork for the anthropologist who possesses, in the ethnographer Evans-Pritchard's words (1962), the capacity "to abandon himself without reserve," "to think and feel alternately as a savage and as a European" and for whom the indigenous society is "in the anthropologist himself and not merely in his notebooks."

Briefly stated, the hypothesis postulated here is that in the course of fieldwork the anthropologist establishes a new object relationship with the culture being studied. Immersion in the alien surrounds of fieldwork induces ego regression in the anthropologist and an outpouring of drive discharges of libido and aggression in the form of transference responses toward aspects of the new object, i.e., the culture and its physical setting. Using Loewald's model of the nature of object relations (1978) I suggest that an internalization of the interactional process of the anthropologist with the object of study may take place, potentially causing psychological change in the fieldworker.

Two sources shall be used in the explication of this thesis; first, Malinowski's (1967) *Diary*, a personal journal that he kept during his ethnographic research; second, the analysis of an anthropologist both before her departure and after she returned from the field.

A DIARY IN THE STRICT SENSE OF THE TERM

Malinowski is a seminal figure in the history of anthropology. His fieldwork, conducted in New Guinea and the Trobriand Islands between 1914 and 1918, led to the publication of his classic monograph, *Argonauts of the Western Pacific*, in 1922. This work, as Clifford (1988) has observed, set the standard for scientific cultural description and ushered in modern ethnography. Malinowski explicitly stated his fieldwork aim as "briefly, to grasp the native's point of view, in his relation to life, to realize his vision of the world." In order to achieve this, he urged the anthropologist "to put aside camera, notebook and pencil, and join in himself in what is going on..." In this endeavor to realize the indigenous person's vision of the world, Malinowski was eminently successful, and his methodology, which Geertz (1988) has referred to as the "total immersion approach to ethnography," has profoundly influenced all later anthropological fieldwork.

Malinowski's personal *Diary* of his fieldwork, discovered among his effects after his sudden death in 1941, was translated from his native Polish and published in 1967. In this work, the rigorous self-scrutiny of the subjective experience of fieldwork dominates the text. Malinowski reveals his intense ambivalence concerning his informants, recounts his mood swings, fantasies, and private thoughts, all leading to what Geertz (1988) has proclaimed "a backstage masterpiece of anthropology, our *Double Helix*." In its candor and intimate detail, the *Diary* paints a vivid picture of the larger problem of observing the "other"; can the subjective be separated from the objective? How much does the observer affect what is being observed and the observed affect the observer? These are epistemological problems the psychoanalyst in the consulting room shares with the anthropologist in the field.

In his original introduction to the *Diary*, Firth, a student and friend of Malinowski, attempts to allay the concerns of impropriety that the publication of such a private and brutally honest document might arouse in the reader. In a second introduction to republication in 1989, he acknowledges with relief its importance to the growing realization that "the position of an ethnographer is not simply that of a recorder of the life of a society, but is also that of someone who both affects that life and is affected by it." He avers that it is "a highly significant contribution to the understanding and role of a fieldworker as a conscious participant in a dynamic social situation."

The *Diary* covers two periods. The first, from September 1914 to August 1915, when Malinowski was working with the Mailu people of New Guinea; the second, from October 1917 to July 1918, which covers most of his last year in the Trobriand Islands. Malinowski is quite specific about the purpose of the *Diary* when he states that he kept it "as a means of self-analysis."

In Brisbane, Australia, even before departing for New Guinea, Malinowski expressed a "strong fear of the tropics; abhorrence of heat and sultriness" (p. 4). This sentiment wells up immediately following a moonlight walk with "a plump blond," the sister of the British Commissioner for New Guinea. The theme of intense desire and equally intense distaste for the setting of his fieldwork, with its obvious sexual connotations, is a recurrent one. As his ship left port, Malinowski relates: "I felt I was taking leave of civilization. I was fairly depressed, afraid I might not feel equal to the task before me" (p. 5).

The rapid alternation of feelings that Malinowski experienced on his arrival is captured in its positive aspect by his lyrical description shortly after arriving: "Felt not too distinctly or strongly, but surely, that a bond was growing up between myself and this landscape. The calm bay was framed in the curving branches of a mangrove tree, which were also reflected in the mirror of the water and on the damp beach. The purple glow in the west penetrated the palm grove and covered the scorched grass with its blaze, slithering over the dark sapphire water—everything was pervaded with the promise of fruitful work and unexpected success; it seemed a paradise in comparison with the monstrous hell I had expected" (p. 10). The negative side quickly emerges in his comment: "Out here the marvelous abysses of verdure are inaccessible, hostile, alien to man. The incomparably beautiful mangrove jungle is, at close quarters, an infernal stinking, slippery swamp … ; where you cannot touch anything. The jungle is almost inaccessible, full of filth—sultry, damp, tiring" (p. 26). His psychological immersion in the setting is vividly symbolized when he encounters a fire in the countryside: "from the hill-side in front of us the fire went on down into the valley, eating at the tall strong grasses. Roaring like a hurricane of light and heat, it came straight toward us, the wind behind it whipping half-burned bits into the air … I walked right into the flames. Marvelous—some completely mad catastrophe rushing straight on at me with furious speed" (pp. 11–12).

Eight days after arriving, Malinowski notes: "at moments was assailed by blackest depression." That night he recounts: "I had a strange dream; homosexual with my own double as a partner. Strangely autoerotic feelings: the impression that I'd like to have a mouth just like mine to kiss, a neck that curves just like mine, a forehead just like mine (seen from the side)" (pp. 12–13). One could postulate that this remarkable dream speaks to a narcissistic regression, a falling back upon the self as a sexual object and comforter in the face of a new and intimidating object relationship with the alien environment. The morning after this dream, Malinowski notes, "I wrote to Mother." A week later he fantasizes about a woman from his past and an interesting contiguity occurs in his *Diary*: "I am still in love with … but not consciously, not explicitly; I know her too little. But physically—my body longs for her. I think of Mother" (p. 16).

Malinowski's intense feelings for his mother while in the field—one manifestation of the regression induced by his isolation in a totally alien setting—are recorded regularly throughout the first section of the *Diary*: "Dream of settling permanently in the South Seas; how will all this strike me when I'm back in Poland? I think—of Mother Self-reproach" (p. 22). Recurrently, Malinowski's romantic memories turn to his mother: "I still think about and am in love with T.—It is the magic of her body that fills me, and the poetry of her presence—all my associations lead in her direction. Moreover, I have moments of general dejection … At last, I begin to feel a deep strong longing for Mother in my innermost being (pp. 27–28). "Occasionally strong yearning for Mother—really if I could keep in communication with Mother I would not mind anything, and my low spirits would have no foundation" (p. 41). Significantly, there is only one incidental mention of his father in the *Diary*, and it is of more than passing interest that, subsequent to his fieldwork, Malinowski published a series of essays disputing the universality of the Oedipus complex.

Malinowski oscillates between the pleasure of his new surroundings and a need to escape back to his recent past: "I would imagine life amid palm groves as perpetual holiday. That was how it struck me looking from the ship. I had a feeling of joy, freedom, happiness. Yet only a few days of it and I was escaping from it in the company of Thackeray's London snobs, following them eagerly around the streets of the big city … I finished *Vanity Fair*—I couldn't tear myself away; it was as though I'd been drugged—I longed to be in Hyde Park, in Bloomsbury" (p. 16).

The constant evocation of sexuality in the tropical situation is captured in the following: "The exoticism breaks through lightly, through the veil of familiar things—an exoticism strong enough to spoil normal apperception, but too weak to create a new category of mood. Went into the bush. For a moment I was frightened. Had to compose myself. Tried to look into my own heart. 'What is my inner life?' No reason to be satisfied with myself. The work I am doing is a kind of opiate rather than a creative expression. I am not trying to link it to deeper sources… Went to bed and thought about other things in an impure way" (p. 31). "Before supper I walked on the veranda and had moments of concentration and spiritual elevation, interrupted by violent surges of sexual instinct for native girls—I dissolved in the landscape" (p. 82).

Feverish and overwhelmed by an intensive data-gathering period Malinowski recounts: "In the evening I was quite *kaput*, I did not read anything. I had moments of wild longings to hear music and at times it seemed to me I was actually hearing it. Yesterday for instance the 9th Symphony—I am still in love with T., and I miss her. I find her body ideally beautiful and sacred, but I realize that physically we had nothing in common, not like Z., for instance. But I am no longer in love erotically with Z. If I could choose one of them as a companion at present, purely impulsively, I would without hesitation choose T… Nevertheless, went to the village— sat and watched women make ramis [grass petticoats] and weave baskets. The rain became more intense. I—inspected a porch filled with little girls, 'there is a fire in the stove' and they were cooking some food. I walked to the street—tired, night fell. The house in transparent gloomy shadows; little streams of water trickling down the middle of the street. Longed for music, for *Tristan and Isolde*. I went back home. For a long time, I couldn't fall asleep. Erotic thoughts—but I believe my monogamous instincts are stronger and stronger—lewdness is beginning to be something alien to me" (pp. 63–65). "Last night I again had a strong attack of monogamy, with aversion to impure thoughts and lusts. Is this because of loneliness and an actual purification of the soul or just tropical madness?" (p. 69).

Episodes of rage erupt frequently as he is faced with the indigenous people's uncooperativeness and venality: "I watched a few dances; then took pictures— but results very poor. Not enough light for snapshots; and they would not pose long enough for time exposures—At moments I was furious at them, particularly because after I gave them their portions of tobacco they all went away. On the whole my feelings towards the natives are decidedly tending to *exterminate the brutes*" (p. 69). On another occasion he recounts his state of "white rage and hatred for bronze-colored skin."

For Malinowski, the physical setting of his fieldwork is female: "in the beauty of a landscape I rediscover woman's beauty or I look for it. A marvelous woman as a symbol of the beauty of nature. Subtle emotional hesitations; search for truth. Struggle for liberation from fetters of sensual pleasure in feeling of beauty—came back in the dark, with Diko. Strong liking for him. Talk about sihari [custom of sitting on the girl's knees]—He shows me what gestures to make to a *kekan* [girl] when they want to *gagai* [engage in sexual intercourse]" (p. 83). The conflict between intense sexual desire for the woman and the simultaneous need to idealize her and purify his feelings can be seen as a frank oedipal manifestation, a theme that is returned to again and again as Malinowski wrestles with carnal impulses in the Trobriand Island section of the *Diary*. By this time (1917) he is engaged to be married (to E. R. M) and he suffers paroxysms of guilt whenever his thoughts or actions become "impure": "Yesterday under the mosquito net, dirty thoughts. Miss H. P.: Miss C. even Miss W.—I thought that even if E. R. M. had been here, this would not have satisfied me. Dirty thoughts about C. R. The doctrine of this man (Ceran) that you're doing woman a favor if you deflower her. I even thought of seducing M. Shook this off—I resolved absolutely to avoid all lecherous thoughts, and in my work to finish the census, if possible today" (p. 156)."—Deep longing. The short *kayaku* [gathering to socialize] in Sugwaywo; young females, blackened with shaven heads, one of them a *nakubukwabuya* [adolescent girl] with an animal-like, brutish sensual face. I shudder at the thought of copulating with her. Thought of E. R. M." (p. 177).

In the Trobriand Island section of the *Diary* his fiancée has become a direct substitution for his mother: "impress of beauty, thought of E. R. M. and whether we'd be able together to wrest beauty of its secret. I am longing for her (moments of longing pierced my screen of sleepy melancholy musing): I felt I wanted her the way a child wants his mother. I thought of Mother" (p. 241). "My everyday reality is permeated with E. R. M. Thought of my marriage—same thoughts when I went to bed, and awakening at night. Identity of this feeling with feelings of child for mother" (p. 245).

Again, the equation of the landscape with "pure" feminine beauty emerges: "A coconut grove, the gently curving bay with its green vegetation which rises like an amphitheatre above. The sand beach—I thought of E. R. M. I feel a mystical link between her and this view, particularly because of the line of breaking waves" (p. 157).

Malinowski's shifting emotional relationship to the object of his investigations is captured in the following: "Suddenly I tumble back into the real milieu, with which I am also in contact. Then again suddenly they stop existing in their inner reality. I see them as an incongruous yet artistic and (savage), exotic—unreal, intangible, floating on the surface of reality, like a multicolored picture on the face of a solid but drab wall" (p. 235).

When he leaves the indigenous culture, he feels dislocated: "it is remarkable how intercourse with whites makes it impossible for me to write the *Diary*. I fall confused into the way of life there. Everything is in the shadow; my thoughts are no longer characteristic in themselves" (p. 244).

The pleasure of immersion in his ethnographic studies is equated with the intense affect of being in love: "Came back, wrote a bit, then went to Kaulaka. Formulated problems, especially those of *kabitam* [craft]— Kaulaka is a poetic village in a long hollow amid palm trees, grove—the pleasure of new impressions—unsettled consciousness, where waves of new things, each with its well-defined individuality, flow from all sides, break against each other, mix, and vanish. A pleasure like that of listening to a new piece of music, or experiencing a new love: the promise of new experiences" (p. 253).

At the end of the *Diary*, Malinowski receives the news of his mother's death. Although overcome by grief and despair, he continues his research but comments: "Everything permeated with Mother" (p. 295). "My own death is becoming something infinitely more real to me—strong feeling—to go to Mother, to join her in nothingness" (p. 297). But finally, he asserts, "At moments I feel that this is only the death of 'something' within me—my ambitions and appetites have a strong hold on me and tie me to life" (p. 298).

A CLINICAL VIGNETTE

The opportunity to examine first-hand the psychological meaning and impact of fieldwork arose through the analysis of a graduate student in anthropology both before her departure and after she returned from the field. Ostensibly, the patient sought analysis because of chronic depression and difficulties with her academic work, but the underlying issues revolved around her traumatic childhood. This background trauma dominated the early part of the analysis and manifested itself in considerable acting out in the first phase of the treatment.

The patient's choice of anthropology as a career was a direct consequence of her traumatic early life. Six months after her birth, her mother became floridly psychotic and was hospitalized. Throughout the patient's childhood and adolescence, her mother sustained recurrent psychotic breakdowns and was often absent from the household for months at a time. Her father's departure from the home on business trips frequently signaled that another maternal decompensation was imminent. Her mother's psychotic episodes, with her father often absent, were terrifying and, on occasion, literally life-threatening to the patient.

Her memories of her childhood were thus of growing up in a phantasmagoric environment where very little was stable and where all hell might break loose at any moment. In the course of analysis, it gradually emerged that the recurrent loss of a predictable "ordinary" mother who became transformed into an irrational, delusional and Medea-like psychotic was a central determinant in her choice of anthropology as a career. She would again experience an environment where familiar social cues did not apply, where the belief system was radically different, and where one could not confidentially predict what might happen next. This time, however, she would master and tame the strangeness and danger of the outside world by studying it, codifying it, and bringing it into the realm of secondary process.

The first part of the analysis, prior to the patient's leaving for fieldwork, was tempestuous and characterized by acting out in the form of many missed sessions. Early on, her identification with her mother and her fear of this identification become apparent. The analytic situation was a chronically frightening one. She had the recurrent thought that she, like her mother, might lose control of her destructive and sexual impulses. Simultaneously, in the transference, I was seen as a dangerous figure like her mother who, through the analysis, might drive her to madness by opening her up like Pandora's box so that all sorts of destructive and uncontrollable demons would emerge.

A further aspect of the maternal transference that appeared was the patient's recurrent view of me as someone who was aloof and uninterested in her. This was revealed to be related to her feelings of emotional deprivation concerning her mother who, through her frequent psychiatric breakdowns and hospitalizations, was absent for long periods of time and, even when physically present in the household, was emotionally unavailable to the patient. The "bad" mother and the "bad" analyst dominated this first phase of the analysis. Although considerable interpretive work was devoted to this issue, the patient's conviction of the analyst as being both potentially dangerous, and simultaneously uninvolved, persisted. The function of this initially unconscious transference was multiple, both distancing me and providing a rationalization for her aggressive acting out. Simultaneously, by casting me in this role, she was able to maintain the fantasy of finding the good "lost" mother through her fieldwork, a fantasy that became conscious as her departure became imminent.

As the time of leaving for the field approached, the patient experienced increasing anxiety. The site she had chosen, a primitive tropical country, brought to mind thoughts of Conrad's *Heart of Darkness* and frightening fantasies of her possible demise by exotic illness or murder at the hands of untamed savages. Simultaneously, however, there was a frankly sexual excitement generated by the thought of the humid, lush, mysterious land she was to depart to. She knew it was common enough for anthropologists in the field to sleep with the indigenous people and this thought was not unattractive to her. At this stage of the analysis, a family romance fantasy emerged. As a child, she had been convinced that she was adopted. The reporting of a dream of a family reunion led to the unveiling of an unconscious fantasy that she would discover her true "good" family in the exotic country to which she was headed. In part, fieldwork was revealed to be a quest for the nurturing good mother.

A hiatus in the analysis of nearly two years transpired before the patient returned from the field. Her reentry into American culture and her return to analysis was emotionally dislocating. She experienced what had previously been familiar as now alien; she felt she did not belong in America, and mourned the loss of her field site. This sense of strangeness about the Western world around her at times bordered on a dissociative state, as if she were observing herself in an exotic setting rather than being back home. The sense of where "home" existed was now in flux. She felt as if the third-world country she had left was now her home.

A prominent feature of the patient's clinical presentation upon her return from the field was the dramatic alteration in the maternal transference, a change that could only be ascribed to psychological shifts that had taken place within the patient during the course of fieldwork. Chronic acting out in the form of missed sessions ceased, and the patient was much more committed to the analysis which no longer was perceived as a potentially dangerous situation. Her self-representation also had undergone considerable alteration—a more stable internal view of herself now existed, and she was no longer as plagued by fears of losing control of her own aggressive and sexual impulses and thus being just like her mother. It was also striking that her intense ambivalence toward her mother had abated. In the period prior to her fieldwork, matricidal fantasies had appeared with regularity and had brought in their train overwhelming guilt and depression. Now she saw her mother for what she was, a pathetic and massively disabled individual for whom she felt considerable compassion. Concurrently, I was now seen as a relatively benign figure who was genuinely interested in her, in contrast to her previous view of me as aloof and, like her mother, potentially dangerous.

In the first part of the analysis, the patient had reported recurrent dreams in which she was being driven somewhere. These dreams almost always possessed an ominous affective tone and, in their manifest content, the feeling that she was being taken to a malignant destination such as Auschwitz. It became apparent that these dreams represented the analysis, with the analyst as driver. Unconsciously, she saw me as a potentially lethal figure who might "drive" her into madness. The childhood memory the dreams were constructed around was of an occasion when she had been with her mother who was driving to meet her father. Her mother was actively psychotic at the time, drove at break-neck speed in the face of her daughter's protestations and terror, and crashed the car. The patient suffered numerous superficial cuts that required medical attention. In the second phase of the analysis, she had a dream of driving a pink Cadillac through a tropical landscape. In her associations, the tropics represented her fieldwork site, and the Cadillac belonged to me; I had given it to her. This gift was the analysis; I had not driven her mad, but I had "driven" her to a type of fulfillment.

The question was thus posed as to which elements, if any, of the experience of fieldwork itself had resulted in such dramatic changes in self- and object representation. Was this simply the resolution of conflicts through action—i.e., being away from the analysis and engaging in living out the fantasy of finding the good mother rather than analyzing it— something that could have occurred in any external context outside of the analysis? Or were there some specific aspects of fieldwork that had promoted these intrapsychic changes?

As the second phase of the analysis proceeded, it became clear, as might be expected, that the seeds of these changes had been laid in the first part of the analysis, particularly the interpretive work that had taken place concerning her identification with her mother. Nonetheless, there were specific aspects of her experience of fieldwork that seemed to have catalyzed these changes. During the early part of her fieldwork, she was assailed by intensely hostile feelings toward the culture she was studying. These feelings were aroused both by the multiple frustrations she encountered in obtaining reliable informants and by the regression that the overwhelming strangeness of the place induced. She became anxious and depressed; nothing seemed to go right. She felt alone and abandoned, confronting an alien and unfriendly, even hostile world. She had recurrent dreams of being back in the welcoming and known confines of the United States. On returning to analysis, she recognized how her rage at her fieldwork site paralleled her feelings about her mother. She had initially wished to be rid of the obdurate and capricious indigenous people just as she had wished to be rid of her mother. She felt totally trapped, immersed in this strange world from which there was no escape. At her first fieldwork site, as she became more fluent in the indigenous language and accumulated pertinent data on the indigenous culture, these murderous fantasies diminished. She began to see the indigenous people and their society in a more benign light. Of central importance in this change was the close relationship she formed

84

with an indigenous informant, a parallel to her relationship with me. While well aware of his frailties and inconsistencies, and often furious at him, she nevertheless began to rely on him more and more, and her work proceeded apace. He was indispensable in helping her obtain the raw data she needed for her thesis. Her perception of the countryside also altered. From being viewed by her as a tropical cesspool, she began to appreciate its strange and dramatic beauty. There was something both terrible and awe-inspiring about both the place and the indigenous customs. She began to dream of the indigenous people as siblings inhabiting her childhood home.

At one of her fieldwork sites, she had formed an intimate bond with an indigenous family and had been formally adopted by them. Her feelings of love for this family, in particular the mother, were intense. She felt she would always belong to them and they to her. She recognized that she had played out her fantasy of finding the good mother, enhanced by this family being among her most important informants. During the last part of her fieldwork, to her surprise, she realized that she felt totally at home, that in some sense she belonged to and loved this place, and she began to feel intense regret at leaving.

In the analysis, it became apparent that in this process of moving from total alienation and loathing of her fieldwork site to a frank love for it and sense of being "at home" there was a counterpart to the shift in her view of the analyst and to some extent of the mother. She had confronted the horror, consciously of the v society, unconsciously of the frightening world created by her mother, and by her anthropological observations brought it into the light of day, mastered it, and made it a part of her. A frank internalization of her interaction with the indigenous society in its benign forms had occurred as was seen in the appearance of her frequent dreams upon returning to analysis of the fieldwork site accompanied by a blissful feeling of "belonging." What seemed to be crucial to this process was the total immersion that fieldwork provided in developing an object relationship with something that was completely "other," alien, frightening, and potentially dangerous, precipitating considerable regression and releasing powerful transference feelings. This was combined with the act of observer, her *raison d'être* for being there, in which she, in a sense, stood outside her immediate subjective experience, examined, studied, and mastered its strangeness—a parallel to the observing ego in analysis. This intense scrutiny provided a type of working through in that over and over again she would examine components of the culture which would at first seem repellent and then would become explicable and more neutral. In so doing, it became apparent through her associations in the analysis that she had unconsciously confronted aspects of both the self and of her mother which to her were ugly and loathsome, and had modified them into a more realistic and benevolent form.

DISCUSSION

The relation of the self (the anthropologist) to the "other" (the foreign culture being examined) in fieldwork is a complex one, possessing some parallels to the analytic situation. As in analysis, fieldwork demands from the anthropologist a total absorption in the task of establishing meaning and bringing coherence to a welter of data much of which may be initially confusing and perplexing. The analyst and the anthropologist are both observers and participants in a process that intimately involves their subjective responses. Emotional vicissitudes for the observer-participant inevitably accompany both ventures. In analysis, not only the analysand, but the analyst, too, may be changed as Freud (1905) eloquently acknowledged when he wrote "No one who, like me, conjures up the most evil of those half-tamed demons that inhabit the human breast, and seeks to wrestle with them, can expect to come through the struggle unscathed" (p. 109).

In fieldwork, unlike analysis, the anthropologist is completely surrounded by the object of study. There is no immediate escape except by retreating, as Malinowski often did, to memories of the home culture that has been left behind. Unlike the analysand, the fieldworker is not accompanied by a guide and interpreter who, to some extent, establishes the "safety" of the analytic situation. It might be contended that the fieldworker is placed in the position of being the "analyst" of those regressive fantasies which are induced in him or her by the encounter with another culture.

Kracke's (1987) account of the psychological effects on him of conducting fieldwork among the Kagwahiv Indians of Brazil is instructive in this regard. He focuses particularly on his transference reactions as he became progressively immersed in Kagwahiv society. Early on, he notes that he experienced a feeling of exhilaration "the excitement of discovery, as I quickly learned basic and important facts about Kagwahiv social culture" (p. 66). This was rapidly followed by "emotional swings between excitement, or idyllic delight, and intense longing for friends and family, home ..." (p. 67). Gradually, he became aware of increasing irritability at not being fully understood by the Kagwahiv, which called to mind a pattern of interaction he had in childhood with a younger sister, strongly tinged with sibling rivalry. His dreams became filled with memories from home and peopled by his family members. He notes, "the dreams themselves grew more intense and primary-process in quality, with affect-laden themes such as hiding from spies" (p. 69), all of which suggested to Kracke a regressive trend induced, in part, by the frustration and disorientation the alien culture aroused. However, more central to this regression, in his opinion, was the rearousal of his experiences of childhood and dependence in response to the situation of having to learn another culture. He relates, "I felt a special affinity with a Kagwahiv much younger than myself—my closest friend was a boy of 16—and with children, partly because they, like me, were having to struggle to learn proper behavior, and would be admonished when they behaved incorrectly" (p. 70). Kracke also observed that it was not only to individual Kagwahiv that he had transference reactions, but also to certain aspects of the culture which evoked them even more strongly. Toward the end of his first period of fieldwork, Kracke was assailed by a pervasive anxiety reaction in response to the free expression by the Kagwahiv of memories of childhood sexual curiosity and childhood oedipal fantasies which were much more readily available to consciousness than they would normally be in Western culture. He notes that, at the time, he was not aware of the extent "to which these interviews with people so much in touch with their fantasies and childhood memories were a vehicle for my getting in touch with these aspects of myself" (p. 76). In the post-fieldwork period, he discovered through his own dreams the extent to which the Kagwahiv expression of these themes became a vehicle for vicarious expression of his own fantasy life, and he thus emphasizes the extent to which aspects of his experience of field work had become internalized.

Loewald (1960) has observed that in analysis a new object relationship is established by the analysand, one that potentially enables development to begin again, a process that, in his opinion, is crucial to therapeutic change. It can be postulated that in the course of fieldwork a new object relationship is established by the anthropologist with the culture being studied such that psychological changes might potentially occur through, to quote Loewald, "the internalization of an interaction process, not simply the internalization of 'objects'" (p. 30).

As in analysis, the situation of fieldwork induces regression, an outpouring of transference responses and some intrapsychic fluidity. Kris (1952) points out that ego regression occurs not only when the ego is weak, but also during many types of creative processes, which would include a scientific pursuit such as fieldwork. He also demonstrates that the "phenomena of ego regression are infinitely more frequent in fantasy than in deliberative preconscious processes [which] suggests that in fantasy the discharge of libido and aggression may have in general a greater proximity to the id—to mobile energy discharges" (p. 312). Kris highlights the relation between creativity and passivity, and suggests that the integrative functions of the ego include self-regulated regression that permits a combination of daring intellectual activity with the experience of passive receptiveness. For the fieldworker, the regression experienced—at least initially—is not self-regulated, but must be tolerated and, to some degree, mastered if true creative ethnography is to be done.

The question has been raised by Herdt and Stoller (1990) in their psychoanalytically oriented ethnographic study conducted in New Guinea as to whether a preliminary analysis should be a central part of the anthropologist's preparation for the field. They conclude in the negative, yet for my patient her analysis preceding fieldwork was of crucial assistance to her in tolerating and using creatively the regression she experienced, while Malinowski felt impelled to keep his *Diary* as a "means of self-analysis." Kracke, too, was able to use his personal experience in analysis to perceptively understand the emotional vicissitudes of his experience in the field. The question of ego flexibility versus ego rigidity concerning the ability to use the regressive experience in the service of the ego is at issue here, and it seems likely that preliminary analysis would, in general, be of great use to the fieldworker in both promoting more ego flexibility and enabling him or her to make creative use of the fantasies that inevitably well up during the engagement with the alien culture.

Fieldwork is not unique in its capacity to induce regression—the student living abroad, the lone sailor or explorer confronting implacable nature or alien places may also experience regressions and confrontations with the self. In fieldwork, however, as in analysis, one is faced with the task of continually attempting to decipher and comprehend one's cognitive and affective responses using one's intellectual and emotional capacities to achieve this goal. It is not inevitable that the anthropologist be psychologically changed by fieldwork since the mobilization of defenses may mute any regression and keep the experience at a "safe" distance. Nonetheless, as Evans-Pritchard (1962) has suggested, in order for a more profound understanding of the indigenous society to be acquired, it must be in the anthropologist himself and not merely in his notebooks. It is my contention that for this to take place, aspects of the interaction process with the object, the Blwl society, are internalized by the fieldworker, an internalization that is a consequence of the regression induced, the subsequent evocation of powerful transference responses, and the working through of them in the act of studying, observing, and codifying the alien society so that some elements of the experience are made a part of the self.

In this regard, the "culture shock" experienced both by Malinowski and my patient upon returning to the culture whence they came is of interest. Malinowski wrote: "It is remarkable how intercourse with whites makes it impossible for me to write the *Diary*. I fall confused into the way of life here. Everything is in the shadow: my thoughts are no longer characteristic in themselves" (p. 244). My patient, on first returning to America, felt a sense of strangeness and alienation parallel to that she had experienced when she first entered her fieldwork site. This, too, gradually dissipated over time, but she was left with the feeling that: "I belong now to two worlds."

Unlike my patient, the factors that led Malinowski to a career in anthropology can only be speculated about, but his peripatetic life before he began fieldwork, his separation from his home as a Polish exile in England, the question of where he belonged, must all have played a part in his interest in alien cultures. His *Diary* suggests an unconscious equation occurred between his romantic feeling for the alien landscapes of his fieldwork and his love for his mother. One could postulate that one motivational element in his pursuit of fieldwork was an unconscious wish to explore and possess the mother's body. As Wax (1990) has observed, Malinowski's later attempt at a refutation of the universality of the Oedipus complex was based on a failure to interpret correctly the data he had obtained in the Trobriand Islands. Wax speculates that Malinowski's critique of Freud's theory of psychosexual development may have owed much to his childhood experience, namely "a long, close and passionate relationship between the young Bronislaw and his mother" (p. 55).

Like Malinowski, Joseph Conrad was also an exiled Pole, one who wandered the world and, in his novels, reworked his experience in exotic climes. Malinowski actually remarked: "Rivers is the Rider Haggard of Anthropology: I shall be the Conrad!" Clifford (1988) has drawn parallels between Conrad's *Heart of Darkness* and Malinowski's *Diary*: "both books are records of white men at the frontier, at points of danger and disintegration. In both sexuality is at issue: both portray an other that is conventionally feminized, at once a danger and a temptation... There is a common thematization of the pull of desire or excess barely checked by some crucial restraint" (p. 105). Conrad has his ambiguous hero Kurtz expostulate, "Exterminate all the brutes," which is self-consciously quoted by Malinowski in a fit of rage when the indigenous people thwart his research.

Conrad captures the potential psychological perils inherent in the regressive pull of fieldwork in the story of Kurtz, who, though an ivory trader, had been charged by the "International Society for the Suppression of Savage Customs" with making a report. Ultimately his immersion in the alien jungle of the Congo overwhelms him: "the heavy, mute spell of the wilderness—that seemed to draw him to its pitiless breast by the awakening of forgotten and brutal instincts, by the memory of gratified and monstrous passions. This alone—had driven him out to the edge of the forest, to the bush towards the gleam of fires, the throb of drums, the drone of weird incantations; this alone had beguiled his unlawful soul beyond the bounds of permitted aspirations—Being alone in the wilderness, it had looked within itself, and, by heavens, I tell you, it had gone mad" (pp. 94–95).

REFERENCES

Clifford, J. (1988).*The Predicament of Culture*. Cambridge, MA: Harvard Univ. Press.

Conrad, J. (1902). *Heart of Darkness*. Harmondsworth, Eng.: Penguin Books, 1978.

Evans-Pritchard, E.D. (1962). *Social Anthropology and Other Essays*. New York: Free Press.

Freud, S. (1905). Fragment of an analysis of a case of hysteria. *S.E. 7.*

Geertz, C. (1988). *Works and Lives: The Anthropologist as Author*. Stanford, CA: Stanford Univ. Press.

Herdt, G. & Stoller, R.J. (1990). *Intimate Communications: Erotics and the Study of Culture*. New York: Columbia Univ. Press.

Kracke, W. (1987). Encounter with other cultures: psychological and epistemological aspects. *Ethos.1558-81.*

Kris, E. (1952). On preconscious mental processes In *Psychoanalytic Explorations in Art.* .New York: Int. Univ. Press, pp. *303–318.*

Loewald, H. (1960). On the therapeutic action of psychoanalysis. *Int. J. Psychoanal.41:16–33.*

——— (1978). Instinct theory, object relations, and psychic structure formation. *J. Am. Psychoanal. Assoc. 26:493–506.*

Malinowski, B. (1922). *Argonauts of the Western Pacific*. London: Routledge.

———. (1967). *A Diary in the Strict Sense of the Term*. Stanford, CA: Stanford Univ. Press, 1989

Wax, M.L. (1990). *Malinowski, Freud and Oedipus. Int. J. Psychoanal..* 17:47–60.

CHAPTER 5

Personal History and the Origins of Psychoanalytic Ideas

John Bowlby And Attachment Theory. By *Jeremy Holmes*. New York: Routledge, 1997, vii + 249 pp., $22.99.

John Bowlby: His Early Life. A Biographical Journey Into The Roots Of Attachment Theory. By *Suzan Van Dijken*. New York: Free Association Books, 1998, Vii + 214 pp., $55.00.

D. W. Winnicott: A Biographical Portrait. By *Brett Kahr*. Madison, CT: International Universities Press, 1996, xxix + 189 pp., $40.00.

Winnicott. By *Adam Phillips*. Cambridge: Harvard University Press, 1988, ix + 180 pp., $15.95.

Fairbairn's Journey Into The Interior. By *J. D. Sutherland*. London: Free Association Books, 1989, xiv + 191 pp., $25.00.

"... we see Planck devoting himself to the most general problems of our science without letting himself be deflected by goals which are more profitable and easier to achieve. I have often heard that colleagues would like to attribute this attitude to exceptional will power and discipline; I believe entirely wrongly so. The emotional state which enables such achievements is similar to that of a religious person or the person in love; the daily pursuit does not originate from a design or program but from a direct need."

—*Einstein*

The influence of personal history, subjective experience, and inner conflict on the origins of psychoanalytic ideas has been a relatively neglected subject. This is striking in view of the recent upsurge of interest in the ways that the analyst's subjective world are important to the clinical situation, and the manner in which the analyst's personal experience influences and shapes the course of treatment. Still, the impact of these factors on psychoanalytic theory building has received much less attention. The appearance over the past decade of a number of comprehensive, psychologically informed biographies of major theoretical innovators in psychoanalysis provides an opportunity to examine this issue. A biographer is subject to personal biases of his or her own that determine what is included or excluded in the telling of a life. This, along with other limitations inherent in biography, inevitably places constraints on what can be concluded about the subjective origins of original ideas in psychoanalysis. However, as these recent biographies demonstrate, there are clear individual elements to be found in the personal histories of some of the seminal thinkers in psychoanalysis that illuminate aspects of their creativity and the provenance of their particular contributions to the field.

Freud's own life history is instructive in this regard. Freud's mother was the third wife of his father, and younger than one of Freud's half-brothers from his father's first marriage. Freud's first playmate was the son of his half-brother, and was a year older than Freud, his uncle. As Gay (1988) has commented, "Such childhood conundrums left deposits that Freud repressed for years and would only recapture, through dreams and laborious self-analysis, in the late 1890s. His mind was made up of these things—his young mother pregnant with a rival, his half-brother in some mysterious way his mother's companion, his nephew older than himself, his best friend also his greatest enemy, his benign father old enough to be his grandfather. He would weave the fabric of his psychoanalytic theories from such intimate experiences" (p. 6). In her penetrating biographical portrait of Melanie

Klein, Grosskurth (1986) observes that Klein grew up in "a family riddled with guilt, envy, and occasionally explosive rages, infused with strong incestuous overtones" (p. 20). She notes that the death of the four-year-old Melanie's sister was "the first of a long series of deaths that punctuated (her) life, each reactivating the original fear, grief, and bewilderment" (p. 15). Among the more important of these losses, Grosskurth relates, was that of her older brother Emanuel, "through disease, malnutrition, alcohol, drugs, poverty, and a will to self-destruction Melanie Klein was made to feel responsible for his death and she carried the guilt with her for the rest of her days" (p. 20). Though Grosskurth does not posit it, I would suggest that this traumatic early life had a profound influence on the development of Klein's theoretical conception of mental life, her preoccupation with aggression, and her view of epigenetic stages wherein concepts of guilt, envy, object loss, and reparation play a dominant role.

Hughes (1997), in a study of Joan Riviere's contribution to our understanding of pathological femininity, has proposed that Riviere's own life experiences are represented in her ground-breaking paper (1929) on that subject. His conclusions are based on two external sources, namely a diary kept by Riviere's mother on her daughter's early childhood, and Riviere's own diary, which she kept prior to becoming a psychoanalyst. Hughes notes that "the pathological femininity that Riviere found in the patient is seen by her as a mask and the women who don it as participants in a masquerade. … She describes a certain type of woman, neither homosexual nor yet fully heterosexual, who uses a kind of femininity to defend against masculine strivings. Masculinity is stolen and must by hidden to avert the reprisals feared if the woman is found to possess it" (p. 901). Through the use of the diaries and other biographical material, Hughes rather convincingly demonstrates that this description applies to Riviere herself, and that her life experiences, especially in relation to men, are directly represented in the paper. In an analogous vein, Geoffrey Cocks (1994), the editor of Heinz

Kohut's correspondence, asserts that Kohut's classic paper *The Two Analyses of Mr. Z* represents Kohut's own two analyses, the first his training analysis with Ruth Eissler in the 1940s, and the second his self-analysis in the 1960s. Though apparently Kohut never informed anyone that he was Mr. Z, Cocks notes that Kohut's wife and son are both convinced that this is the case.

In a recent book review, Marcus (1998) observed: "Part of the inner meaning of important writings is to be traced in how they emerge obliquely from ostensibly distant or remote personal experiences." And further: "Our understanding of the structure of even an abstruse argument can be augmented by an informed sense of personal urgings, impulses that are bound up though indirect and often unacknowledged means to larger events in the world." The books under review here tend to substantiate Marcus's contention concerning the catalytic effect of personal experience on the provenance of original ideas.

John Bowlby (1907–1990) is best known as the creator of attachment theory. Formally trained as a psychoanalyst, Bowlby was at one point Deputy President of the British Psychoanalytic Society, and he viewed attachment theory, with its wedding of ethology and psychoanalysis, as a means of placing object relations theory on a scientific basis. Perhaps because of his emphasis on scientific observation and methodology, his work received a chilly reception within traditional and conservative psychoanalytic circles of the time. As Holmes (1993) has observed: "In rejecting Bowlby, his psychoanalytic critics felt that by restricting himself to a narrow definition of science—to what could be observed and measured—Bowlby was missing the whole point of psychoanalysis. Any so called 'science' of the mind which did not take account of the inner world of phantasy was worthless and certainly had no place within psychoanalytic discourse" (p. 4). This repudiation of his work is perhaps best exemplified by the Kleinians' response to the famous film he made with James Robertson, which showed graphically the distress exhibited by a two-year-old who was separated from her parents when she had to go into the hospital. As Holmes recounts: "The Kleinians in the audience (at its showing at the British Psycho-Analytic Society) were unimpressed and felt that the girl's distress was due more to her unconscious destructive phantasies towards her pregnant mother's unborn child than to the separation itself" (p. 4). Nevertheless, Bowlby's work on separation and maternal deprivation was found to be clinically compelling, reached a huge audience, and spawned much important research which continues to this very day.

Bowlby's interest and awareness of the impact of separation on children's development had a long history, and antedated his formal training in psychiatry and psychoanalysis. In 1929, at the age of 22, Bowlby worked at Priory Gate School, an educational institution for maladjusted children. Suzan van Dijken in *John Bowlby: His Early Life* quotes him as saying: "And when I was there, I learned everything that I have known it was the most valuable six months in my life" (p. 48). Following graduation from medical school and while finishing his psychoanalytic training, Bowlby began work in 1936 at the London Child Guidance Clinic, where he treated and studied children with persistent behavior problems. His research on the origins of delinquency led him to conclude in 1940 that "in a large number of these cases the child's bad character can be traced unequivocally to prolonged separation from mother (or mother substitutes) in early childhood" (p. 110).

The publication in 1951 of his World Health Organization monograph *Maternal Care and Mental Health*, which sold some 400,000 copies in English alone, established his reputation. As van Dijken points out, it was while working on this monograph that Bowlby became aware that there was no existing theory to explain his findings on the profound effects of separation experiences on young children: "what was missing in that monograph was how comes it that those experiences could possibly have those effects" (p. 5). Simultaneously, he was introduced to Lorenz's work on imprinting in non-human species. Lorenz had demonstrated that, in some species of birds, bonds developed between the newly hatched bird and a mother figure entirely as a consequence of exposure to the presence of the mother, and not as an outgrowth of feeding behavior.

These ethological findings deeply influenced Bowlby, and in his seminal 1958 paper "The Nature of the Child's Tie to His Mother" he postulated that attachment behavior in humans was distinct from feeding and sexual behavior, and possessed equal primary significance. This was in opposition to classical psychoanalytic theory, wherein the infant's attachment was viewed as a secondary consequence of the mother's provision of experiences of instinctual gratification. As Holmes has indicated, Bowlby had hoped that attachment theory would illuminate and strengthen object relations theory, but the opposition, even hostility, from orthodox psychoanalysis led to attachment theory, although it owed much to psychoanalysis, becoming a discipline in its own right. (One British analyst is quoted by Grosskurth as saying caustically: "Bowlby? Give us Barrabas!") The current status of attachment theory within the broader rubric of psychoanalysis is beyond the scope of this paper, but Holmes, one of its foremost contemporary champions, recognizes its limitations in ignoring the power of fantasy, while observing that Bowlby's emphasis on the importance of the environment as a determinant of psychopathology appears to have been vindicated on many fronts.

Van Dijken's study of Bowlby attempts to find the personal roots of Bowlby's interest in separation. She traces his private and intellectual life up until 1951, and identifies a number of significant separation experiences in his childhood which, she avers, sensitized him to the theme that was to dominate his creative life. Bowlby's father was a prominent and successful London surgeon who received appointments as Royal Surgeon to Edward VII and George V, and a knighthood. Sir Anthony Bowlby was known as a strong personality who never wavered in his clinical convictions or ideas, an attribute that his son John shared. Bowlby's mother was of aristocratic lineage, being the granddaughter of the Welsh peer Lord Mostyn. Bowlby was the fourth of six children; he was born when both of his parents were already middle-aged.

As was typical in upper- and middle-class Edwardian families, the Bowlby children saw their mother for only a short, circumscribed time each day, and they saw even less of their busy father. The children's care was the business of a nanny, who was aided by nursemaids. On summer holidays in Scotland, however, Bowlby's mother shared with her children her love of nature, teaching them to identify flowers, birds, trees, and butterflies. This love of nature remained with Bowlby throughout his life, and, one could speculate, made him particularly receptive to the ethological findings that were to provide the intellectual backbone for attachment theory. The Bowlby family nursemaid Minnie was fondest of John, for whom she cared from birth, but she left the household when John was only four. Later in life he wrote: "for a child to be looked after entirely by a loving nanny and then for her to leave when he is two or three, or even four or five, can be almost as tragic as the loss of a mother" (p. 26). With the outbreak of the First World War in 1914, Bowlby's father left for the front, and was home only rarely until he returned from active service in 1919. Emotionally distant and professionally occupied before the war, he was, to all intents and purposes, completely absent for its duration. In 1918, John and his slightly older brother Tony were sent to a preparatory boarding school outside of London. John appears to have been quite unhappy there, and van Dijken recounts that he once told his wife that he would not send a dog to boarding school at that age. Similarly, she notes (p. 34) that in his book *Attachment and Loss* Bowlby quoted Graham Greene's feelings about boarding school, reflecting his own bitterness: "Unhappiness in a child accumulates because he sees no end to the dark tunnel. The thirteen weeks of a term might just as well be thirteen years."

At the age of fourteen, Bowlby entered the Royal Naval College at Dartmouth where, interestingly in light of his later fascination with Lorenz's work, he became an avid bird-watcher and avian photographer. In 1924, he began training as a midshipman assigned to a ship of the Atlantic Fleet. Though he enjoyed naval life, he decided that such a career was limiting, and he entered Cambridge University as a preclinical medical student at the age of 18. As part of his course work, he engaged in a considerable amount of study in evolutionary biology, a subject that was to remain of abiding interest to him. (Bowlby's last major published work was a psychobiography of his great exemplar, Darwin). At Cambridge, Bowlby received a rigorous education in the natural sciences. His tutor was the distinguished physiologist Lord Adrian, who was sympathetic to Freudian theory; he felt it "went far beyond a single range of facts; it showed or tried to show quite unexpected relations between different fields." This summary statement is equally applicable to Bowlby's own work.

Van Dijken (p. 11) notes that Bowlby commented on the effect his childhood had on him by stating that he had been "sufficiently hurt but not sufficiently damaged," and that close colleagues stated: "We speculated that John's own early experience must have included a degree, if not of actual deprivation, of some inhibition of his readiness to express affection" (p. 11). The loss of his beloved nanny at four, his father's total absence during the First World War, and his mother's relative remoteness, together with the final indignity and trauma of being sent away to an impersonal boarding school, not only led to what others characterized as his protective shell of not sharing his feelings, but also sensitized him to the profound psychological impact of separation experiences on the vulnerable child. This personal history, combined with his experience as a teacher of maladjusted children and his immersion in the natural sciences, all nurtured a fertile mental field for the growth of his major intellectual achievement, attachment theory.

Donald Woods Winnicott's invention and explication of such evocative concepts as "good-enough mothering," the "holding environment," the "transitional object," and the "false" self has garnered for him an enduring fame that extends, as Esman (1990) has noted, far beyond psychiatry and psychoanalysis and into our culture at large. Within British psychoanalysis, Winnicott (1896–1971) was the standard-bearer for the Middle Group that attempted to find common ground between the bellicose Freudian and Kleinian camps. His *Collected Papers* were appropriately subtitled *Through Paediatrics to Psychoanalysis*, since he never relinquished his identity as a pediatrician even after he completed psychoanalytic training, and indeed he retained his position as a pediatric consultant at Paddington Green Children's Hospital in London for some forty years. He described himself as "a psychiatrist who has clung to pediatrics." His immersion as a pediatrician in the treatment of innumerable mother-infant dyads contributed to the famous aphorism "There is no such thing as a baby"—a statement which Esman feels spelled the death-knell to any one-person psychology of human development or mental functioning.

In a perceptive review of the evolution of Winnicott's thought, Modell (1985) observes that Winnicott loved paradox, and once stated: "What you get out of me, you will have to pick out of chaos." Undeterred, Modell chronicles the gradual unfolding of Winnicott's creative journey. He observes that Winnicott was preoccupied with the interplay between inner and outer reality, particularly "the interplay of edges." Modell also notes that Winnicott emphasized the healing potential of regression, which he understood not only as a retreat to chaos, but also as an attempt at cure. The idea of transitional phenomena, which was perhaps his most original concept, further advances his dominant creative theme, which, as Modell relates, "concerns a fundamental problem for human psychology as well as philosophy—the relation between the subject and the self-created object, the relation between the subject's inner world and what is outside" (p. 125). Modell also highlights Winnicott's awareness of the profound significance of play and playing: "He is in tune with the historian of culture Huizinga who observes that the essence of play is its freedom, that play is not trivial but leads us to very deep subjects indeed, such as the nature and origin of religious concepts" (p. 127). Or, as Winnicott himself said,

> "Psychotherapy takes place in the overlap of two areas of playing, that of the patient and that of the therapist. Psychotherapy has to do with two people playing together." In this regard, it is of interest that Clare Winnicott (1978), in her brief and poignant memoir of her husband, stated, "The essential clue to D. W. W.'s work on transitional objects and phenomena is to be found in his own personality, in his ways of relating and being related to, and his whole life style. What I mean is that it was his capacity to play which never deserted him, that led him inevitably into the area of research that he conceptualized in terms of the transitional objects and phenomena" (p. 18).

In Freud's case histories, mothers receive short shrift, and the patients' relationships to their fathers are seen as central to an understanding of their psychopathology; this undoubtedly reflects the patriarchal society of Freud's Vienna as well as Freud's personal prejudices and life experience. In Winnicott's work the opposite is true; fathers become virtually invisible. As Phillips (1988) has commented, "Fathers tend to turn up in his writing in brackets or parentheses." This emphasis in Winnicott's theoretical corpus on the primacy of the mother and the subsidiary importance of the father in the child's development is firmly rooted in Winnicott's personal experience.

Winnicott was the third and youngest child of his parents, and the only son. His father was a highly successful merchant in the provincial English coastal town of Plymouth, and the Winnicott family lived in comfortable circumstances. In his later years, Winnicott's father was active in local politics (twice becoming Lord Mayor of Plymouth), civic affairs, and religious activities in the Wesleyan Church, all of which culminated in his receiving a knighthood in 1924. His mother was the daughter of a local pharmacist, and she maintained a traditional upper-middle-class role in running her household and a home in which she took great personal pride. Significantly, Winnicott wrote in a notebook that he kept just prior to his death: "Now my sisters were older than I, 5 and 6 years; so, in a sense I was an only child with multiple mothers and with a father extremely preoccupied in my younger years with town as well as business matters" (C. Winnicott 1978, p. 23). Kahr (1996), in his biography of Winnicott, shows that the household also included an aunt, a nanny for Donald, and a governess for his sisters, as well as a cook and several parlor maids. As Kahr further demonstrates, apart from a ten-minute stroll with his father every Sunday after services at the local Methodist Church, Winnicott spent virtually all his time in the presence of women. Kahr concludes that this immersion in an all-female world led to a powerful female identification: "First of all because young Donald received so much affection from so many women with whom he interacted in a reliable manner, he felt protected, safe and secure, and this emotional stability provided him with a solid foundation for a sturdy, protective and creative adult life. Secondly, the preponderance of women in Winnicott's childhood stimulated an extreme fascination with the inner world of the female.... He devoted more than forty years of research to the explanation of motherhood and to the examination of the child's relationship with the mother" (p. 6).

About his father Winnicott rather revealingly commented: "So my father was there to kill and be killed, but it is probably true that in the early years he left me too much to all my mothers. *Things never quite righted themselves*" (C. Winnicott, p. 24; emphasis added). Phillips picks up on this statement to suggest that: "It is not the father that interests Winnicott as coming between the mother and child to separate them, but a transitional space from which the father is virtually absent and which initially joins and separates the baby and the mother" (1988, p. 28). Phillips further observes that in his paper "The Capacity to Be Alone" (1958), Winnicott states that this capacity is dependent upon and begins with the child's experience of being alone in the presence of the mother. However, he omits the equally significant experience of being alone in the presence of the father.

Kahr and Phillips both suggest that Winnicott's rather shadowy mother suffered from depression, and that the direct experience of a depressed mother had a profound impact upon Winnicott. They both quote a poem he wrote at the age of 63, entitled *The Tree*, which contains the following:

Mother below is weeping weeping weeping
Thus I knew her
Once, stretched out on her lap as now on dead tree I learned to make
her smile to stem her tears to undo her guilt to cure her inward death
To enliven her was my living

Kahr postulates that this early experience of ministering to a sad mother prompted Winnicott to care for other sad individuals. He wrote: "Analysis is my chosen job, the way I feel I will best deal with my own guilt, the way I can express myself in a constructive way."

Phillips comments that Winnicott, a Methodist churchgoer during his youth, wrote in the same plain language that John Wesley, the founder of Methodism, both praised and displayed when he said in the preface to his *Sermons*: "I design plain truth for plain people." However, Winnicott's "plain" language is deceptive and, as in poetry, layers of meaning and allusion, and elliptical, paradoxical comments can make some of his writing maddingly difficult to understand. In the end, his work is worth the intellectual effort required of the reader. In some ways Winnicott, the genius-poet of psychoanalysis, establishes an area of play between himself and the reader: that same transitional space that he both created and discovered in his female-dominated childhood home in Plymouth.

Ronald Fairbairn (1889–1965) has posthumously emerged from the shadows of comparative obscurity to recognition as one of the most original and penetrating thinkers in the history of psychoanalysis. His ascent to this pantheon has come about through a burgeoning awareness of the centrality of his ideas to the current theoretical ferment in psychoanalysis. For instance, the recently born "relational" psychoanalysis, with its emphasis on the interaction between patient and analyst as the crucial agent of therapeutic change, is hugely indebted to Fairbairn's legacy. Much of what Fairbairn wrote anticipated Kohut. Robbins (1994) has delineated the "almost uncanny" resemblance of Kohut's self psychology to Fairbairn's object relations theory (while acidly noting that Fairbairn is nowhere cited as a reference in Kohut's two major books). Kohut and Fairbairn also share one singular aspect of personal history —that they were both only children.

Fairbairn, living in Edinburgh, relatively isolated from the larger analytic community, was a radical theorist. In a series of papers beginning in 1940, he created an object relations model of developmental psychology and pathogenesis which repudiated classical drive theory. His now-famous rallying cry for this conceptual frame declared: "The object and not gratification is the ultimate aim of libidinal striving" (Fairbairn 1943, p. 328). Ernest Jones (1952), in a perceptive and appreciative introduction to Fairbairn's *An Object Relations Theory of the Personality*, captured the essence of his thesis: "If it were possible to condense Fairbairn's new ideas into one sentence, it might run somewhat as follows. Instead of starting, as Freud did, from stimulation of the nervous system proceeding from excitation of various erotogeneous zones and internal tension arising from gonadic activity, Fairbairn starts at the center of the personality, the ego, and depicts its strivings and difficulties in its endeavour to reach an object where it may find support" (p. v). Recent commentaries on Fairbairn's ground-breaking work (Grotstein and Rinsley 1994; Scharff and Birtles 1994) adumbrate his theoretical views, so I will not recapitulate them here except to highlight certain essential features, particularly the view that libidinal development depends upon the degree to which objects are incorporated, and the nature of the methods used to deal with incorporated objects. For Fairbairn, psychopathology is conceived in terms of the disturbance of object relationships during development, and not in terms of intrapsychic conflict between id and ego. In his theory of therapy, Fairbairn conceives of the psychotherapist as an exorcist who casts out devils (the bad objects) by providing himself as a powerful good object who gives the patient sufficient sense of security to allow the terrifying bad objects to emerge slowly into the light of day. Religious metaphors pervade Fairbairn's writing, reflecting an early desire to become a clergyman. This was eventually transmuted into the decision to train in medicine with a view to becoming a psychotherapist since, he felt, in such a vocation, as in the ministry, issues of conscience, guilt, sin, and sexuality could be directly addressed. In Fairbairn's cosmos, the metaphors of religion and psychology overlap: "there is now no doubt in my mind that the greatest source of resistance is fear of the release of bad objects from the unconscious for when such bad objects are released, the world around the patient becomes peopled with *devils* which are too terrifying for him to face."

J. D. Sutherland, an analysand of Fairbairn, wrote *Fairbairn's Journey into the Interior,* an unusually intimate biography based on a thirty-six-year personal relationship, and access to Fairbairn's diary and the notes of his self-analysis. The far-reaching and revealing nature of Sutherland's account is perilously close to what Malcolm (1995) has acknowledged as the transgressive nature of biography,[1] but Sutherland confronts the issue of potential impropriety. He defends his text on the grounds that Fairbairn himself had often commented on the intimate interplay of theoretical preferences and personality features in all scientific theorizing, therefore indirectly giving his imprimatur to Sutherland's remarkable study.

William Ronald Dodds Fairbairn was the only child born into a prosperous, middle-class, late-Victorian Scottish household. His father was a successful property valuer and surveyor, staunchly Presbyterian, who married in his early thirties. His mother was an Englishwoman who, Sutherland notes, was "strict to the point of being a martinet in bringing up her son to conform to the formalities of their class, religious and otherwise." She was prone to frequent illnesses, and the household, according to Sutherland, was permeated with her Victorian taboo on sex. Nonetheless, "she conveyed her conviction to her son that he was unusually gifted and with a special future which she wished him to realize" (p. 64). While Fairbairn was a child, his father developed the symptom of being unable to urinate in the presence of others, a symptom that began to plague Fairbairn himself in the 1930s; his attempts to treat it by self-analysis in the late 1930s led directly to his theoretical formulations.

Fairbairn attended an elite private school as a day pupil, but his father vetoed the proposal that he should go on to Oxford on the grounds that it was a place of suspect morality. Fairbairn therefore enrolled at Edinburgh

---

[1] Malcolm acerbically comments that "The voyeurism and busybodyism that impel writers and readers of biography alike are obscured by an apparatus of scholarship designed to give the enterprise an appearance of banklike blandness and solidity." And further: "The reader's amazing tolerance (which he would extend to no novel written half as badly as most biographies) makes sense only when seen as a kind of collusion between him and the biographer in an excitingly forbidden undertaking: tiptoeing down the corridor together, to stand in front of the bedroom door and try to peep through the keyhole" (p. 9).

University, from which he graduated with honors in philosophy. Imbued with the religious fervor that had been an outgrowth of avid adolescent attendance at services—Presbyterian ones in Scotland and Anglican ones when visiting his English relatives—he decided to become a clergyman. Prior to embarking on his divinity courses, he pursued Hellenic studies abroad. When the outbreak of the First World War interrupted his theological studies, he served as an officer in the British Army's campaign in the Middle East, participating in Allenby's victory over the Turks in Palestine. The war was a defining event for Fairbairn, and his experiences in it precipitated in him a new interest in medical psychology. Sutherland feels that a phobic anxiety that Fairbairn had developed at the prospect of preaching sermons was another factor contributing to his career change. By 1923, Fairbairn had graduated from medical school, and he spent the next two years as a house officer at the Royal Edinburgh Hospital, the center of psychiatric training in Scotland.

Fairbairn married in 1927 at the age of thirty-seven, but by the 1930s difficulties had begun to emerge in his marriage, and his wife was complaining bitterly about the time he devoted to his professional life. By 1934, Fairbairn had become, in Sutherland's word, "possessed" by an inhibition about urinating in the presence of others, which curtailed his freedom to travel. Sutherland postulates that Fairbairn's wife's destructive attitudes toward his work had led him to a defensive identification with his father, who had been able to assert himself against being controlled by his wife, but whose "masculinity was deeply and mysteriously linked to his phobia of urinating in the presence of others" (p. 36). In some measure, this symptom of Fairbairn's, and its association with his father, can be seen as a direct personal experience that eventually generated one of the central concepts in his theory of the inner object world, that of the "internal saboteur."[2]

On the basis of self-analytic notes that Fairbairn recorded just prior to his period of intense creativity in the 1940s, Sutherland contends that Fairbairn's experience as an only child, in perpetual closeness to repressive and ambivalently perceived parents, led directly to his conception of the "basic endo-psychic situation," with its somewhat Ptolemaic metapsychology of rejecting, exciting, and ideal objects, all linked to corresponding parts of the original ego.[3] Sutherland recounts that throughout 1939 Fairbairn had become increasingly preoccupied with his schizoid patients, some of whom were excessively demanding in their dependence upon him. He suggests that Fairbairn's persistent urinary symptom must have been causing increasing travail at this time, and that in parallel with his own personal symptom, sadistic urination fantasies were becoming ever more prominent in one of his patients. This set the stage for Fairbairn's self-analysis, which resulted in the conviction that internalized object relations were central to an understanding of psychopathology. Sutherland feels that Fairbairn's highly ambivalent relationship with his mother had established a severe inhibition of his sexuality, and that much of the affect in this childhood situation had been revived by his wife's strident hostility to his work. Just after World War II broke out, and stimulated by his debilitating urinary symptom, Fairbairn began a systematic study of his childhood, and wrote careful self-analytic notes. He recorded: "Having irritation of foreskin and telling Mother who put vaseline on foreskin. Wondering why it was all right

---

[2] The "internal saboteur" represents one element of Fairbairn's theory of the universal splits that occur in the original ego structure during development. It denotes a "rejecting object" that is tied to the self in a relationship of primitive identification.

[3] Sutherland summarizes Fairbairn's theory of the "basic endo-psychic situation" as: "an original ego structure split into: (a) a central ego, the 'I'; (b) a libidinal ego; and (c) an aggressive persecutory ego.... In addition to the relationships of each sub-self with the central self, the two sub-selves have a reciprocal and powerfully dynamic relationship with each other" (pp. 125–126).

for Mother to touch my penis and not for me to do it. ... Evidently it was a case of being all right when authorized by Mother, but *fatal* otherwise" (pp. 66–67).

Sutherland views these private notes as free associations showing the development of a dominant internal figure in Fairbairn's childhood—a severe mother attacking dirty or disorderly behavior. He comments: "An overall impression from this first group of notes is of the screen. I was on the same side of newspaper screen as Father. It was an appalling experience. Father seemed in great pain and had the greatest difficulty in passing water.... He 'sweated blood.' It was like seeing Christ on the Cross. I was closely identified with Father in the experience. I was on his side of the newspaper screen and I wanted to urinate very badly too. I watched the scene aghast. I was terribly sorry for Father. It seemed awful to be unable to urinate when you wanted to so badly and to be confronted with the danger of one's bladder bursting (a danger which Father had often dwelt upon to me)" (pp. 70–71).

Sutherland postulates that during this period of self-analysis Fairbairn became aware of splitting in the unity of his self (one of his key theoretical ideas), and of the internalization of a persecutory bad mother as a dominating internal object. The incident on the train was profoundly traumatic, and Sutherland suggests that he identified with his father as if he himself were being crucified. Out of the drama of this self-analysis sprang the seminal paper "Schizoid Factors in the Personality." He began to delineate his theory of the endopsychic world with its array of good and bad objects—a central conscious ego attached to the ideal object, a repressed libidinal ego attached to the exciting object, and a repressed antilibidinal ego attached to the rejecting object. These theoretical creations are intimately connected to Fairbairn's heroic self-analytic odyssey into the interior world as he tried to understand and conquer his crippling urinary symptom.

Alongside the private inner journey laid bare by Sutherland, Fairbairn's rigorous university training in philosophy is germane to an understanding of one of his more controversial postulates: namely that normal human relationships are fundamentally interpersonal and not, like their pathological equivalents, internalized. Scharff and Birtles (1994) have drawn attention to the significant influence on Fairbairn of Hegel, who saw desire as essentially unsatisfying. This dissatisfaction leads to a need to control the object, and hence to the need to transform and own that object, a position that Fairbairn embraced in his object relations theory. Fairbairn lived his whole life in Edinburgh, which had also been the home of the great eighteenth-century empirical philosopher David Hume. Interestingly, Hume in his philosophical writings completely repudiated the idea of the self, whereas Fairbairn made the emergence of the self the center of his life's work. Fairbairn was steeped in the independent intellectual tradition of the Scottish Enlightenment that Hume exemplifies, and immersed in the intense and often discordant parental attention that only children receive. He forged an original concept of the nature of the mind that derived directly from the internalization of his childhood experience with an intrusive, puritanical mother and a suffering, "crucified" father. His self-analysis, melded with his rigorous training in philosophy and theology, enabled him to forge a theoretical structure that has transformed the landscape of psychoanalysis.

Discussion

Philosophers of science have long acknowledged that our theoretical models of the nature of the world are, at best, mental approximations of reality filtered through the interpretation of the available data, the historical context, and the personal biases of the creator of the theory. Nowhere is this more true than in the universe of psychoanalysis, where new conceptual models and theories often become focal points for sectarian disputes and ideological battles, where objectivity gets lost, and where intimations of apostasy and heresy all too sadly predominate. With the passage of time (and sometimes the demise of the most fiercely zealous antagonists), a more sober view of the validity and clinical utility of once-reviled ideas takes hold. Schafer's (1994) recent account of the theoretical views and clinical practice of contemporary Kleinians, which demonstrates areas of congruence and overlap with more traditional Freudian perspectives, speaks to this type of reconciliatory development over time.

The issue of context—personal, historical, and cultural—is especially germane to the development of psychoanalytic ideas. As one example of the profound impact of cultural influence and themes, Kirschner (1996) has convincingly demonstrated how psychoanalytic theories of the development of the self have direct ancestors in Western religious and Romantic narratives, all of which attempt to delineate, address, and make meaningful the most difficult existential issues that human beings face.[4] She shows that the basic form of the Judeo-Christian narrative, which chronicles man's creation, fall, and potential redemption via reunion with God, has a secularized variant, that Kirschner calls the Romantic spiral, or *Building*, in which religious terms are recast into natural and secular ones: "instead of being a story about the soul, it is a tale of the mind's estrangement from nature and gradual development towards reintegration with nature at a higher level" (p. 10). Kirschner further proposes that Romanticism provided a vocabulary from which psychoanalytic theorists drew—an explanation

---

[4] Kirschner posits that the transmutation of spiritual narrative into psychological theory took place over the centuries that coincided with the secularization of our culture. As she observes: "A key transitional period in the history of that secularization was the Romantic era. Romanticism was the great pivot-point in Western spiritual history. In the years immediately following the American and French revolutions, numerous artists and thinkers ... translated key religious themes and values into non-theological terms. The "soul" was refigured as the "mind" or the "self" and God receded from view" (pp. 1-2).

that I have also suggested for the culture of subjectivity that pervades much modern psychoanalytic thinking (Buckley 1997). Kirschner feels that "the psychoanalytic development narrative highlights the tension between fusion and separation—a tension that heralds the birth of the self and continues to affect its development thereafter. It is the story of a progression from an originally undifferentiated unity, through a painful but necessary chain of ruptures, losses and differentiations, towards a culmination … in which the severed elements are reunited, by means of an integration that preserves their differentiated distinctiveness. Since it entails movement from 'lower' to 'higher' forms of unity, it is considered to be an inherently good and valuable developmental process. It is derived from a root narrative that has existed for many centuries" (p. 94). For Kirschner, the forms of "redemption" to be found in psychoanalytic developmental theory—intimacy, authenticity, even the process of internalization—are secular versions of an ancient inherited spiritual code that provides their template.

Psychoanalysis, since its inception a century ago, has been firmly rooted in the wellsprings of subjective experience, and the many factors from within and without that determine that experience. An examination of the influence of personal experience on the provenance of original ideas, such as the biographies of Bowlby, Winnicott, and Fairbairn reviewed here provide, does not diminish the importance of their insights. On the contrary, it enhances a more objective perspective; it allows a greater appreciation of their creativity, and of the validity of their conceptions of certain aspects of psychological functioning and structure. An exegesis of the inner forces that generate original ideas does not reduce the value of those ideas; it enhances an understanding of their context, and an appreciation of the complex, sometimes heroic, struggle that leads to their birth. The history of psychoanalysis has all too frequently been bedeviled by a fallacious and fractious reductionism, wherein the part comes to dominate the whole. A broader contextual analysis helps to oppose that tendency. It also facilitates a more objective integration of innovative And insightful concepts into the evolving and dynamic mosaic that makes up modern psychoanalysis.

REFERENCES

Buckley, P. (1997). Psychoanalysis And Its Romantic Rebellion. *J. Amer. Psychoanal. Assn.*45:577–579.

Cocks, G. (1994). *The Curve of Life: Correspondence of Heinz Kohut, 1923–1981.* Chicago: University of Chicago Press.

Esman, A.H. (1990). Three Books by and about Winnicott. *Int. J. Psycho-Anal.*71: 695-699.

Fairbairn, W.R.D. (1943). The repression and return of bad objects. *Brit. J. Med. Psychol.*19:327–341.

Gay, P. (1988). *Freud: A Life for Our Time.* New York: Norton.

Grosskurth, P. (1986). *Melanie Klein: Her World and Her Work.* Cambridge: Harvard University Press.

Grotstein, J.S. & Rinsley, D.B., Eds. (1994). *Fairbairn and the Origins of Object Relations.* New York: Guilford Press.

Hughes, M. A. (1997). Personal Experiences—Professional Interests: Joan Riviere And Femininity. *Int. J. Psycho-Anal.*78:899–911.

Jones, E. (1952). Preface. In W.*R.D. Fairbairn, Psychoanalytic Studies of the Personality.* London: Tavistock Publications, pp. *v–vii.*

Kirschner, S. R. (1996). *The Religious and Romantic Origins of Psychoanalysis.* Cambridge: Cambridge University Press.

Malcolm, J. (1995). *The Silent Woman: Sylvia Plath and Ted Hughes.* New York: Vintage Books.

Marcus, S. (1998). Review of *Isaiah Berlin: A Life,* by Ignatieff M. *New York Times,* Book Review Section, November 29.

Modell, A.H. (1985). The works of Winnicott and the evolution of his thought. *J. Amer. Psychoanal. Assn.33:113–137.*

Riviere, J. (1929). Womanliness as a masquerade. In *The Inner World and Joan Riviere: Collected Papers, 1920–1958,* ed. A. Hughes. London and New York: Karnac Books, pp. *90–101.*

Robbins, M. (1994). A Fairbairnian object relations perspective on self psychology. In Fairbairn and *the Origins of Object Relations,* ed. J.S. Grotstein & D.B. Rinsley. New York: Guilford Press.

Schafer, R. (1994). The Contemporary Kleinians of London. *Psychoanal Q.63: 409–432.*

Scharff, D. E., & Birtles, E. F., Eds. (1994). *From Instinct to Self: Selected Papers of W. R. D. Fairbairn.* Northvale, NJ: Aronson.

Winnicott, D. W. (1958). The Capacity to be Alone. *Int. J. Psycho-Anal.39: 416–420.*

Winnicott, C. (1978). *D.W.W.: A reflection. In Between Reality and Fantasy,* ed. S. A. Grolnick & L. Barkin. New York: Aronson.

CHAPTER 6

Experiencing Madness

Elyn R. Saks's *The Center Cannot Hold* (2007) and Kay Redfield Jamison's *An Unquiet Mind* (1995) are exemplars of a psychiatric confessional genre—first-person accounts of severe mental illness. Such narratives are manifold and extend back to classical antiquity. In the second century C.E., the Roman sophist Aelius Aristides wrote of his psychosomatic illness and its treatment. According to Rosen (1968) this was the first autobiographical account of mental illness. Some have made their authors famous. Daniel Schreber, a prominent 19th century German jurist developed a mid-life psychotic illness which led to his hospitalization for nine years. During the latter part of this period he published, to the dismay of his family, a memoir of his illness and treatment (Schreber, 1903/1955). His text indicates that he remained floridly psychotic. Freud (1911/1971) would use Schreber's book as the scaffolding for his theory of the psychodynamics of paranoia and the mechanism of projection thus providing Schreber with enduring recognition (at least in psychoanalytic circles).

To this reader, what is compelling about Saks's and Jamison's memoirs, alongside the authors' considerable literary talent, is an unflinching honesty concerning the subjective horrors of their illnesses. They are unsparing in describing the relentless, recurrent invasion of their rational minds by their psychoses. They are candid about the treatment, or lack of it, they received or repudiated. It is of interest to psychiatry to examine what was actually therapeutic for them and enabled them to not fatally succumb and to be able to enjoy ongoing productive and creative professional lives. It has to be acknowledged that both these authors are unusual people—intellectually gifted, capable of withering introspection, ambitious and, as their books demonstrate, able to use their traumatic personal experience of psychosis by writing about it. Not your average patient with severe, crippling mental illness. Nonetheless, certain elements of what helped them stand out and may have more general implications for therapeutic endeavors with the psychoses.

Saks is a professor of law at the University of Southern California. From her adolescence onwards she regularly fell apart psychologically. While in law school at Yale she was hospitalized, delusionally convinced that: "There will be raging fires and hundreds maybe thousands of people lying dead in the streets. And it will all—all of it—be my fault" (Saks, 2007, p. 4). She felt her hospitalization was "a brutal experience" (Saks, 2007, p. 6) because of the use of restraints and forced medication. (Some years later she wrote a scholarly text advocating for the civil rights of the mentally ill.) Despite recurrent, life-threatening psychotic episodes, Saks resisted for many years the belief that she had schizophrenia and suffered from a real illness. After multiple treatment failures her experience with an effective antipsychotic broke apart this denial:

"The clarity that *Zyprexa* gave me knocked down my last remaining argument. There's no way to overstate what a thunderclap this revelation was to me. And with it, my final and most profound resistance to the idea that I was mentally ill began to give way. Ironically, the more I accepted I had a mental illness, the less the illness defined me—at which point the riptide set me free" (Saks, 2007, p. 304).

Saks had many tempestuous, but generally helpful and sometimes lifesaving engagements with psychotherapists:

Medication has no doubt played a central role in helping me manage my psychosis but what allowed me to see the meaning in my struggles—to make sense of everything that happened before and during my illness, and to mobilize what strengths I may possess into a rich and productive life—is talk therapy.—It is at the heart of things, a relationship and for me it has been the key to every other relationship I hold precious (Saks, 2007).

By the time Jamison wrote her memoir she was the coauthor of the standard text on manic-depressive illness. When she was 28:

I was manic beyond recognition and just beginning a long, costly personal war against a medication that I would, in a few years' time, be strongly encouraging others to take. My illness and my struggles against the drug that ultimately saved my life and restored my sanity had been years in the making (Jamison, 1995, p. 4).

Jamison's first attack of manic-depressive illness occurred when she was a senior in high school. The ecstatic aspects of her mania were intoxicating: "I felt great. Not just great, I felt really great. I could do anything" (p. 36). "The inevitable down-turn was horrifying: 'my mind' had turned on me—it no longer found anything interesting or enjoyable or worthwhile.—I was going to die, what difference did anything make—why live?" (p. 38). These excruciating cycles recurred throughout college and into her academic life. They are limned by her with evocative writing: . you are irritable, angry, frightened, uncontrollable and enmeshed totally in the blackest caves of the mind. You never knew those caves were there. It will never end, for madness carves its own reality" (p. 67). She notes:

… mania is not a luxury one can easily afford. It is devastating to have the illness and aggravating to have to pay for medications, blood tests and psychotherapy. They, at least, are partially deductible. But money spent while manic doesn't fit into the Internal Revenue Service concept of medical expense or business loss. So after mania, when most depressed, you're given excellent reason to be even more so (p. 75).

The efficacy of effective combined psychopharmacology and psychotherapy is captured by Jamison:

At this point in my existence I cannot imagine leading a normal life without taking lithium and having had the benefits of psychotherapy. Lithium prevents my seductive but disastrous highs.… But, ineffably, psychotherapy heals. It makes some sense of the confusion, reins in the terrifying thoughts and feelings, returns some control and hope of possibility of learning from it all. Psychotherapy is a sanctuary; it is a battleground; it is a place I have been psychotic, neurotic, elated, confused and despairing beyond belief. But, always, it is where I have believed—or have learned to believe that I might someday be able to contend with all of this (p. 88–89).

What can be gleaned from these two inspirational stories of living with ravaging mental illness? Not simply the obvious that skilled use of medication and psychotherapy works best (true in both cases). Saks and Jamison highlight the profound blow to their self-esteem and their identity that their illnesses engendered. Their initial intense desires to deny being ill is a common phenomenon in those who experience psychosis. Ultimately, it was healing [for them] to embrace the disease as part of themselves and not to sequester it as an alien invader. Saks (2007) observes: "My good fortune is not that I have recovered from mental illness. I have not nor will I ever. My good fortune lies in having found my life" (p. 336). Jamison (1995) notes: "The Chinese believe that before you can conquer a beast you must first make it beautiful. In some strange way, I have tried to do that with manic-depressive illness, It has been a fascinating, albeit deadly, enemy and companion" (p. 5). As these two memoirs suggest, bringing the demons of psychosis into the light of day, making the "enemy" a "companion," a dangerous one who needs to be constantly monitored, is itself therapeutic and helps to temper the profoundly demoralizing narcissistic injury that psychotic illness inevitably brings in its wake.

REFERENCES

Freud, S. (1911):A psychoanalytic notes on an autobiographical account of a case of paranoia. *Standard Edition* 12:1–82.

Jamison, K.R. (1995). *An unquiet mind.* New York: Alfred A. Knopf, Inc.

Rosen, G. (1968). *Madness in society.* New York: Harper & Row.

Saks, E.R. (2007). *The center cannot hold.* New York: Hyperion.

Schreber, D.P. (1955). *Memoirs of My Nervous Illness.* I. MacAlpine & R.A. Hunter Eds. & Transl.. London: Dawson and Sons. (Original work published 1903)

SECTION TWO:
CULTURAL INTERFACES

CHAPTER 7

The Hammer of Witches

The virulent epidemic of witch-hunting that erupted in Europe during the late 15th century has remained the subject of much interest to social historians, perhaps in part because of its disquieting parallels with the persecution and genocide that have been such a prominent and sordid part of our own century. And indeed, commonalities may be seen in the psychology of persecution of a scapegoat group in times of social unrest and dissatisfaction, even with respect to specific accusations levelled against such groups across the centuries. Thus, for instance, two of the main crimes levelled against witches, ritual murder and cannibalism, were also charged against early Christians themselves in the Roman Empire, against the Knights Templars when they were crushed by Philip IV of France, and against the Jews in the *Protocols of the Elders of Zion* in our own era. However, one aspect of the witch-hunts that differentiates them from other outbursts of persecution is the prominence of women as victims. This aspect in particular invites psychoanalytic scrutiny.

The witch-hunts arose at the close of the medieval period and the beginning of the new era of Reformation and Renaissance, persisting over a period of two hundred years, after which they sputtered out. The world of the late Middle Ages was characterized by a pervasive sense of unease and impending doom in which such symptoms of psychic turmoil as bizarre millenarian movements, processions of flagellants, and epidemics of mass hysteria swept over Europe. As Huizinga has eloquently said: "At the close of the Middle Ages a somber melancholy weighs on peoples' souls. Whether we read a chronicle, a poem, a sermon, a legal document even, the same impression of immense sadness is produced by them all. It would sometimes seem as if this period had been particularly unhappy, as if It had left behind only the memory of violence, of covetousness and mortal hatred, as if it had no other argument than that of intemperance, of pride, and of cruelty."

The sense of emotional dislocation has been seen to reflect the fact that that society was undergoing radical changes. Feudalism was crumbling and being replaced by the nascent nation state. Both social and religious rebellions were occurring; in particular the Catholic Church was losing authority as the prolonged stress of the Black Death contributed to a loss of faith, and as a result of the rise of Protestantism. Thus, the atmosphere was created for the reassertion of social control through the victimization of an out-group symbolizing new, i.e., "heretical," forces. The trials and executions of witches organized by the ecclesiastical authorities, both Catholic and then Protestant, and supported by the secular power, provided a chilling example to the populace at large of the fate that would befall all heretics, i.e., rebels.

The theoretical document that provided the intellectual catalyst for the witch-hunts was the *Malleus Maleficarum* written by two Dominican priests, Kramer and Sprenger, and published in 1484. This tract was widely disseminated and used as a handbook for the identification and destruction of witches. In it was forged the necessary recruitment of local peasant beliefs in black magic that had existed harmlessly for centuries to an overriding conception of an empire of witches under the dominion of Satan, epitomized by Satanic sexual congress at orgiastic sabbeths which were sacrilegious parodies of divine service. While the reasoning of this tract is scholastic, its tone is anything but unemotional. Its tortuous arguments are conveyed in an atmosphere of threat, anger, and vilification. Theological arguments are amply supplemented by anecdotes and cautionary tales. In its anecdotes and diatribes are expressed a wealth of fantasy material relevant to the psychoanalytic understanding of misogyny, and perhaps a key to why the singling out of women for persecution in this era was so felicitous a choice that the witch-hunts lasted for such an extended time.

Some have postulated that the belief in witchcraft was not irrational and a delusion, but in fact made good sense. This view was based on the fact that Europe in the Late Medieval and Post Reformation periods had experienced the overwhelming stresses of both the Black Death and the Reformation, that a dualistic view of a titanic struggle between good and evil was universally accepted, and that the calamities and horrors of life then could more reasonably be ascribed to the agency of Satan and his legions than to mere chance. A more parsimonious social explanation can be found by observing that the *Malleus Maleficarum* was an ecclesiastical doctrine, and that the Catholic Church was under assault on many fronts. In the face of its loss of authority, the *Malleus* can be seen as the blueprint for a reign of terror which had social control as its primary motive, and hence, was one manifestation of a larger attempt by the Church to maintain its power.

Witchcraft belief has caught the imagination of analysts from the beginning. The most systematic explication of the *Malleus* has been attempted by Jones. He concludes that the witch belief represented "in the main an exteriorisation of the repressed sexual aspects of women, especially those related to the feminine part of the infantile oedipus situation." He sees the dichotomy between witch and Virgin Mary as equivalent to the little boy's dissociation of the father into God and devil images. He observes that the terror of the witches *maleficium* (harmful magic) was derived from a fundamental fear concerning the failure of sexual function, and he notes that the *Malleus Maleficarum* devotes considerable attention to the various ways in which the penis is "bewitched away." Symbolic representations of sterility, for instance, witches, can effect the destruction of crops through conjuring up hail storms as well as render arable land infertile, are equated by Jones to castration anxiety. Jones's analysis of the witch belief certainly captures the

Malleus's preoccupation with sexual dysfunction and fear of sterility, but it is remarkable that he views the witch idea largely as an externalization of the genital conflicts of women. Related to this view, he believes that one of the major explanations for the rise of the witch frenzy at the close of the 15th century was the state of widespread jealousy and dissatisfaction among women due to the depletion of the male population in the incessant warfare throughout Europe during this period. Interestingly, this is consonant with the authors of the *Malleus* who state that the most powerful motivation of women's evil is rivalry. This view completely overlooks the fact the ideas of witchcraft were codified and promulgated by men, the trials and executions organized by men, and the necessary support for the witch-hunts, both secular and ecclesiastic, came entirely from men. For the male, according to Jones, the fear of oedipal punishment is also the dominant force behind witchcraft belief, with the fear belonging to the father somehow transferred to woman. Hence the fear of witchcraft owes its real force to fear of the devil. Thus, in this view it is almost incidental that it is women who must be attacked by men in witch-hunts.

Zilboorg has also addressed the psychoanalytic issues raised by the *Malleus*. He emphasizes its anti-erotic aspect, which, of course, is not new to the 15th century but represents a traditional aspect of medieval Catholicism and thought. He sees the conflict between ascetic authority and the increasing hedonism of the age as precipitating a severe paranoid mass psychosis. Here, it is woman as erotic temptress that is the basis of misogyny.

On the level of manifest content, the hatred of women evident on every page of the *Malleus* ("For what else is woman, but a foe to friendship, an inescapable punishment, a necessary evil, a natural temptation, an admirable calamity, a domestic danger, a delectable detriment, an evil of nature, painted with fair colors?") is justified in terms of the female as instigator of base sexual urges. They state the power of the devil "lies in the privy parts of men," and in answer to why are women so much more likely to ally themselves with the devil than men, they answer that woman is "more carnal than men." They even (erroneously) derive the very word woman to mean "lust of the flesh." A reason is provided for the predominance of women as Satan's agents: "All witchcraft comes from carnal lust which is in women Insatiable." Other contributing characteristics of women that make for their ready adherence to witchcraft are their superstition, immoderation of emotions, ambition, vanity, etc., etc. These accusations are traditional. However, it is our contention that this diatribe is fueled by even more primitive and powerful feelings of envy and narcissistic mortification.

The *Malleus Maleficarum* is divided into 3 parts. The first establishes the existence and defines the concomitants of witchcraft. The second provides what amounts to "clinical" examples of maleficium and its treatment. The third deals with the judicial procedures for uprooting witches, including their arrest, interrogation, torture and execution.

At the very beginning, the authors are concerned to establish the existence, ubiquity, and power of witches. The important point is that this required a modification of medieval Catholic theology. Though the official ecclesiastic recognition of witchcraft began in the 5th century with St. Augustine, the position of the medieval Church was that witches were to be regarded as figments of human fantasy, and that it was un-Catholic, essentially pagan, to attribute vast supernatural agency to them. Now this sober, secondary-process view is rejected. The authors acknowledge that many of the activities or effects ascribed to witches may be illusory, for instance, "demons cannot actually effect any permanent transformation in human bodies" or "the penis does not actually disappear but may be perceived as gone," but they dismiss this as irrelevant. They argue that the fantasy of having performed unnatural acts is just as much proof of the nefarious activity of Satan and the reality of witches as if actual unnatural events had occurred: "It is useless to argue the end result of witchcraft may be a fantasy and not reality because such a fantasy cannot be procured without resort to the power of the devil." And further: "Since the devil has extraordinary powers over the minds of those who have given themselves up to him, what they do in imagination, they believe they have actually and really done in the body." Their obliteration of the importance of distinguishing between fantasy and reality (and their occasional loss of awareness of their own acknowledgement of illusion, as when for instance they describe as concrete the basket of penises collected by a witch) as insisted upon by the medieval fathers, amounts to a frank ego regression to the level of omnipotence of thought. They conclude that to *disbelieve* in witches is the heresy.

Kramer & Sprenger's ubiquitous preoccupation with the sexual insatiability of women is followed In the *Malleus* by a concern over the vulnerability of the sexual function of men. Women are portrayed as voracious lustful creatures dominated by their instincts, capable of any vice and cupidity whereas men are sexually fragile: "the reason why more men than women are bewitched in respect of that action—such obstruction generally occurs in the seminal duct, or in an inability in the matter of erection, which can more easily happen to men; and therefore more men than women are bewitched." One of the main crimes that witches are accused of is that they may work some "Prestidigitory illusion so that the male organ appears to be entirely removed and separate from the body." This frank castration fantasy is a recurrent theme throughout the Malleus. The authors acknowledge that it may be done by illusion but state that "It Is not illusion in the opinion of the sufferer, for his imagination can really and actually believe that something is not present since by none of his exterior senses, such as sight or touch, can he perceive that it Is present" (a further obfuscation of fantasy and reality). Case examples are provided in the second part of the *Malleus* in one of which male organs are collected in great numbers by witches. In another, when a lover wishes to leave his mistress he "lost his member, that is to say, some glamour was cast over it so that he could see or touch nothing but his smooth body." Witches are also accused of causing less dramatic sexual difficulties than frank castration, such as impotence and blockage of the seminal vessels, thus preventing ejaculation.

An Intriguing "psychological" argument is offered by the authors in the second part of the *Malleus* to explain the means by which the legions of Satan "deprive man of his Virile Member: All these things are caused by devils through an Illusion or glamour in the manner we have said, by confusing the organ of vision, by transmitting the mental Images in the imaginative faculty. And it must not be said that these members which are shown are devils in assumed members, just as they sometimes appear to witches and men in assumed aerial bodies, and converse with them. And the reason is that they effect this thing by an easier method, namely by drawing out an inner mental image from the repository of the memory, and impressing it on the imagination."

The *Malleus* catalogues other ways in which witches injure mankind. They blaspheme against God, cause destruction of goods, interfere in marital relations, and kill children. However, the connection with hatred for women with their capacity of childbearing emerges from the overwhelming preoccupation with the subject of birth. This preoccupation takes the form of direct accusations against witches for their powers and their hostile attitudes in regard to birth as well as a plethora of phantasies depicting impregnation and birth in pregenital psychosexual modes, and thus rendering them bisexual rather than feminine functions. Both devices reveal a tremendous degree of envy of female generative capacities In this context male sterility cannot be simply reduced to symbolic castration but reflects the same issue.

Typical examples of phantasies in which generation and delivery are detached from women and/or rendered in pregenital modes (such as ocular, urinary, and anal) are the following:

1. *ocular germination.* The devil is "able to collect various germs or seeds and able to cause various species to glow by looking at them."
2. *anal birth:* "And he (male wizard) at once took off his clothes and went into the stream, not standing up but sitting with his back against the current; and while the others looked on, he uttered certain words, and moved the water with his hands behind his back, and in a short time he brought out a great quantity of butter."

In addition, there Is a major discussion of the question "whether children can be begotten by devils" which specifically states that the devil may take "both active and passive" roles (i.e., they are first transformed Into a succubus with a vagina who receives a man's semen and then turn into an incubus with a penis who can copulate with the witch and generate a child.) Thus, the sexual capacities of both male and female are combined in one figure.

Even more striking, when women are pictured as pregnant or parturiciant, they are attached in phantasies that show them as horrible, and treat the contents of the womb as fecal matter (or mock the process of delivery as productive of nothing). Thus, "a pregnant woman when she wanted to perform an action of nature, all those unclean things fell from her body, thorns, bones, bits of wood." Or again, "when the time of parturition comes, their swelling (supposed pregnancy) is relieved by no more than the expulsion of a great quantity of wind." Yet again, "a pregnant woman whose belly touched by a witch gave birth not (even) to an entire abortion but, little by little, to separate fragments of it—head and feet and hands." The destruction of the contents of the mother's womb, according to Klein, an expression of envy of the mother's pregnancy and good insides, could not be more vivid.

Particular enmity toward midwives is another theme that expresses hostility toward the woman with powers in regard to birth. She is treated as the most baneful of her sex and the likeliest to be corrupted by witchcraft. Her opportunity to abort a fetus or harm the newly born child, or claim it for the devil, is dwelt upon. The authors make the fierce and sweeping claim, "No one does more harm to the Catholic Faith than mid-wives."

The connection between these fantasies of destruction and feelings of envy does not escape the authors. It appears in projected form. They state specifically that witches in these instances are motivated by a profound envy of the fruitfulness of others, and that in general it is in women's nature to be envious.

It is curious that the projection involved in seeing women as sexual has been noted, while the projection involved in seeing them as envious (of other's fruitfulness) has been overlooked. Interestingly, most of the women prosecuted as witches were older women who had been married and widowed, rather than spinsters.

In this context, it is noteworthy that women are also associated with death: "I have found a woman (to be) more bitter than death."

Van Leewuen has noted that women's receptiveness, as well as their ability to bear children, have long been underestimated as sources of envy in the male.

In her opinion, this envy is based upon the man's inability to create a baby. The inability of some males to renounce the possibility of childbearing, accompanied by intense envy of the female in procreation and nurturance has been described as a problem in development by Jacobson, Kubie, Boehm, Klein, Rosenfeld, and others. Freud described pregnancy phantasies in boys and men but made no mention of the envy of women. The envy of men for women's ability to bear children has been studied by Jacobson.

She found this to be a particularly active theme in male patients with latent homosexual problems whose feminine traits hinged around an intense envy about women's ability to grow and produce children. In the *Malleus,* women are constantly accused of profound envy of others' fruitfulness which can be viewed as a frank projection of the authors' envy of women's procreative ability.

Mack Brunswick has noted that in preoedipal development, the boy has to sacrifice his wish to grow babies, just as the girl has to renounce her desire for a penis. The authors of the *Malleus Maleficarum* seem to have never achieved this necessary renunciation of feminine wishes for pregnancy and a child.

Boehm felt that the wish by men to possess feminine characteristics was a function of their concealed envy of the larger penis which women are imagined to possess. He felt that death and castration wishes toward the mother in pregnancy were not simply rage against the coming sibling, but were due to the envy of the mother's condition. He felt that boys and girls imagined that the man loses his penis, which is then incorporated into the woman who hides it away and turns it into a child. In the *Malleus Maleficarum* this fantasy of the penis being bewitched away and hidden is quite explicit. Zilboorg, in his study of Couvade ceremonies, concluded that men's envy of the woman is larger than women's envy of the man. He interpreted Couvade as a manifestation of man's tremendous jealousy of the woman mother who is undeniably superior in her childbearing. Nurnberg also noted the relationship of birth fantasies in men to castration and death fears, and this connection seems quite clear in the *Malleus Maleficarum.*

In the present case, the question is why should a universal conflict become central and powerful—and exploitable—at the time it did?

Probably the most significant emotional "event" of the period was the recurrent epidemics of Bubonic Plague, which destroyed about one third of the population of Europe, and in many communities, as much as half the population. It was called "the Great Dying." In addition, marauding bands of brigand soldiers roamed the countryside in the intervals between actual outbreaks of war, further ravaging the population. Death was a sudden and constant accompaniment to life. This must have caused a profound sense of helplessness which stimulated compensatory strivings for omnipotence. These strivings emerge in the *Malleus*, first in the regression in form of thinking to omnipotence or thought (elevating fantasy to equal status with reality); second in a preoccupation with the seemingly magical act of childbirth and envy of women's reproductive power; and thirdly, in the arrogation of god-like powers over life and death implicit in the blueprints for capturing and ruthlessly punishing witches. Moreover, the rage that accompanied the assault on (collapse of) infantile omnipotence by the ever-present losses and reminders of mortality seem to have fueled an unconscious link between women as the life-givers, and women as the takers and threateners of life. In this period, the personification of death in European painting changes from a male figure to a female.

Unconsciously, women's ability to create life may have become associated with the calamitous mortality that had overtaken society. As part of their diatribe against women, the authors of the *Malleus* emphasize the relationship of women and death: "And I have found a woman more bitter than death—more bitter than death than the devil. For though the devil tempted Eve to sin, yet Eve seduced Adam. And as the sin of Eve would not have brought death to our soul and body unless the sin had afterwards passed to Adam to which he was tempted by Eve, not by the devil, therefore she is more bitter than death." Predicated on fantasies that were as present in ancient Greece in the myths of the Sphinx, Medusa, Medea, and the Furies, as in the 15th Century, a lethal assault on women at this time can be viewed as a response to the pervasive presence of sudden death and the profound sense of helplessness that this evoked.

135

Huizinga has captured the temper of the times when he says, "... a general feeling of impending calamity hangs over all. Perpetual danger prevails everywhere....The background of all life In the world seems black. Everywhere the flames of hatred arise and injustice reigns. Satan covers a gloomy earth with his somber wings."

The response to this preoccupation with death seems to have been an attack upon the life-givers, women, in a furious paranoid assault fueled by an underlying envy of women that can be viewed as a reaction to the helplessness and collapse of unconscious infantile omnipotence that the ever-present spectre of death evoked in the male populace.

REFERENCES

Brunswick, R.M. (1940). The preoedipal phase of the libido development. *Psychoanal. Quart.* 9:293–319.

Freud, S. (1909). Analysis of a phobia in a five-year-old boy. *S.E.* 10.

——— (1918). From the history of an infantile neurosis. *S.E.* 17.

Jacobson, E. (1950). Development of the wish for a child in boys. *Psychoanal . Study Child.* 5139–152.

Jones, E. (1951). *On the Nightmare.* New York: Liveright.

Klein, M. (1957). *Envy and Gratitude: A Study of Unconscious Sources.* New York: Basic Books.

Kubie, L. (1974). The drive to become both sexes. *Psychoanal. Quart.* 43:349–426.

Van Leeuwen, K. (1966). Pregnancy envy in the male. *Int. J. Psychoanal* .47:319–324.

Kramer, H. & Sprenger, J. (1484). *Malleus Maleficarum* (transl. M. Summers). London: Pushkin Press, 1948.

Zilboorg, G. (1935). *The Medical Man and the Witch During the Renaissance.* Baltimore: Johns Hopkins.

——— (1944). Masculine and feminine; some biological and cultural aspects, *Psychiatry* 7:257–296.

CHAPTER 8

Ancient Templates:
The Classical Origins of Psychoanalysis

In dreams

> the beastly and savage part (of the mind) endeavors to sally forth and satisfy its own natural instincts ... there is nothing it will not venture to undertake as being released from all sense of shame and all reason. It does not shrink from attempting to have intercourse with one's mother, or with any man, god, or animal. It is ready for any foul deed of blood ... and falls short of no extreme of mindlessness and shamelessness ... there is in every one of us, even those who seem to be most moderate, a type of desire that is terrible, wild and lawless.

While one might confidently assume that the preceding passage was written by Freud, it is startling to discover that it was composed by Plato two and a half millennia ago and appears in his masterpiece The Republic (1). Freud paid Plato appropriate homage by calling him "divine," but interestingly asserted that his knowledge of Plato was fragmentary. Bergmann,[1] however, has demonstrated that Gomperz's Greek Thinkers, with its extensive sections on Socrates and Plato, was cited by Freud as one of his favorite books. Further, Freud translated into German, John Stuart Mill's 1866, 67-page article on Plato. Freud, like many original thinkers, is not alone in denying intellectual ancestors and as a final convincing piece of evidence of the link between Plato and Freud, Bergmann juxtaposes a quotation from Plato with one from Freud. In Phaedrus (2) Plato states:

> I divided each soul into three—two horses and a charioteer; and one of the horses was good and the other bad: the right-hand horse is upright and cleanly made; he has a lofty neck and an aquiline nose; his color is white; his eyes dark; he is a lover of honor and modesty and temperance; and the follower of true glory; he needs no touch of the whip, but is guided by words and admonition only. The other is a crooked lumbering animal, . he has a short thick neck; he is flat-faced and of dark color; with gray eyes and bloodred complexion; the mate of insolence and pride, shaggered and deaf, hardly yielding to whip and spur. Now when the charioteer beholds the vision of love, and has his whole soul warmed through sense, and is full of the pricking and tickling of desire, the obedient steed, then as always under the government of shame, refrains from leaping on the beloved; but the other, heedless of the pricks and blows of the whip plunges and runs away, giving all manner of trouble to his companion and the charioteer. (pp. 253—254)

In *The Ego and the Id* (3), Freud wrote:

> In its relation to the id, it is like a man on horseback, who has to hold in check the superior strength of the horse: with the difference that the rider tries to do so with his own strength while the ego uses borrowed forces. The analogy may be carried a little further. Often a rider if he is not to be parted from his horse, is obliged to guide it where it wants to go; so the same way the ego is in the habit of transforming the id's will into action as if it were its own.

> The ego represents what may be called reason and common sense, in contrast to the id, which contains passions. All this falls in line with the popular distinction which we are all familiar with.... (p. 25)

Bergmann suggests that Freud's term, popular distinction, can be used as a denial of the Platonic origins of this metaphor. Notwithstanding Freud's abjuration of any debt to Plato, it is clear that this ancient Greek philosopher anticipated the creator of modern psychodynamic theory when he articulated in The Republic a conflict model of the psyche in which instinctual drives represent a constant threat to rational behavior.

Some years ago, Simon (4) demonstrated the presence of three main models of mind in ancient Greece, elements of which remain with us in contemporary psychotherapeutic and psychiatric practice. The first of these conceptual models Simon labeled the poetic (mainly Homeric). In the Homeric model there is no clear idea of mental structure, and, as in many preliterate societies, mental illness is viewed as something "sent" by wrathful gods from outside the individual. To some extent this would correspond with our contemporary sociocultural model of mental illness originating in external pathogenic forces impinging on the individual. It is also one, shorn of its animistic elements, which is used by contemporary family therapists, among others, in their therapeutic endeavors.

The second model found in classical Greece is the Hippocratic, the comparatively unmodified ancestor of our current biomedical model. A classic example of this ancient Greek biological model of mental illness occurs in Hippocrates' discourse on epilepsy:

> It is thus with regard to the disease called Sacred; it appears to me to be nowise more divine nor more sacred than other diseases, but has a natural cause from which it originated like other afflictions. Men regard its nature and cause as divine from ignorance and wonder,

because it is not at all like other diseases. And this notation of its divinity is kept up by their inability to comprehend it (5, pp. 334–335).

In the Corpus Hippocraticum, the brain was recognized to be the source of the emotions:

And men ought to know that from nothing else but thence come joys, delights, laughter and sports and sorrows, griefs, despondency, and lamentations. And by the same organ we become mad and delirious, and fears and terrors assail us, some by night, and some by day, and dreams and untimely wanderings, and cares that are not suitable, and ignorance of present circumstances, desuetude and unskillfulness. All these things we endure from the brain when it is not healthy (5, 344).

The third ancient Greek model of the mind and the one germane to this essay is the Platonic or philosophical model. Simon observes that "It is fair to say that much of Plato's philosophical activity was involved in the task of defining and characterizing the nature of the psyche (mind)." And further "we can look at Plato as the one who defined the abstract and the rational as equivalent to the moral good. He equated self-knowledge with self-restraint, and proclaimed that knowledge is virtue.... Lack of knowledge and the irrational, were equated with moral evil, and then, with madness. " Plato divided the psyche into three parts, the rational, affective, and appetitive and again Simon observes that "here conflict is conceptualized as a struggle between the rational and the appetitive portions with each trying to enlist the affective portion on its side. " Thus, we have an early tripartite view of the mind that echoes Freud's later structural model of ego, id, and superego. Plato saw mental illness as a consequence of an imbalance whereby the unbridled instinctual part gains the upper hand. Treatment is through the

Platonic dialogue, a precursor of the psychoanalytic dialogue that brings the conflicting parts of the mind into harmony and reasserts control over the irrational part of the psyche. The philosophical dialogue, however, differs radically from the psychoanalytic dialogue, by attempting to discard the emotions, whereas in the analytic dialogue emotions are at the center of the treatment.

Jonathan Lear, a philosopher and a psychoanalyst, has drawn parallels between philosophy and psychoanalysis in his book Open Minded: Working out the logic of the soul (a title that is itself derived from Plato). Lear states (6):

Psychoanalysis, Freud said, is an impossible profession. So is philosophy. This is not a metaphor or a poetically paradoxical turn of phrase. It is literally true. And the impossibility is ultimately a matter of logic. For the very idea of a profession is that of a defensive structure, and it is part of the very idea of philosophy and psychoanalysis to be activities which undo such defenses. It is part of the logic of psychoanalysis and philosophy that they are forms of life committed to living openly—with truth, beauty, envy and hate, wonder, awe and dread. The idea of a profession of psychoanalysis or a profession of philosophy is thus a contradiction in terms. Or to put it bluntly, there is no such idea. (p. 5)

He further comments:

It is only to say that a certain activity which Plato called "giving a logos of the psyche" has all but disappeared. An everyday way of rendering the Greek is "working out the logic of the soul." In the twentieth century it has become difficult to understand this phrase because the remarkable advances in formal logic since 1879 have so colored our understanding of what logic is. We lose sight of Plato's project, laid out so beautifully in the Republic, of giving a nonformal but rigorous, not-quite-empirical yet not nonempirical account of what it is to be human. Plato, one might say, is working out the very idea of what it is to be minded as we are. And he does this in the light of Socrates' exemplification—a life spent showing—that one of the most important truths about us is that we have the capacity to be open minded: the capacity to live nondefensively with the question of how to live. (p. 8)

Lear notes that "in The Republic, Plato invents psyche-analysis though he posits that Plato is more concerned with the vicissitudes of narcissism than Freud ever was." Lear also suggests, rather extravagantly in my opinion, that Plato invents object-relations theory: he understood that the human psyche is in dynamic interaction with the cultural political environment, and that both are fundamentally shaped by the movement of meanings from polis to psyche and back again. He works out one of the most insightful accounts of psychosocial degeneration ever formulated. Contemporary object-relations theorists, if they go back to Plato, will study his account of psychopathology with awe. For Plato, the influence of polis on psyche or of psyche on polis is largely unconscious. And human life is, for the most part, lived in the midst of illusion. In Plato's famous image of the cave, we are, unbeknownst to ourselves, strapped to a wall and forced to watch the projections of images onto the opposite wall which we mistake not only for reality, but for ourselves. We are, on this account, strangers to ourselves. But for Plato as for Freud, there is therapeutic potential in pushing hard at contradictions inherent in the illusions themselves. Every image is a shadow, a distortion of something bearing more reality than it. In focusing on the distortion we can painfully and slowly work our way toward what the distortion is a distortion of. Once again Plato plants the hope of avoiding despair. (6, p. 10)

It should be noted that Simon (4) has a highly original interpretation of Plato's cave and its shadows:

> If we review [Plato's] lists of the characteristics of the baser and higher parts of mind and now consider the last proposition— Plato's denigration of sexual differences and intercourse as a method of begetting and creating—a rather simple but remarkable construction occurs. Consider the items in the list; flux; sleep and dreaming; conflict; begetting, being born, and perishing; and heterosexuality—do these add up to any one simple unifying construct? I propose that they do, and that we can best see that unity by thinking in terms of a particular childhood experience and its fantasy concomitants—a primal scene fantasy … "one of the central allegories in (the Republic), the myth of the cave, is, of course, built around the contrast between shadowy darkness and bright light … Interwoven with the imagery of night and the imagery and theme of sexuality." (pp. 171, 172, 176)

In Plato's proposal that children must not know their biological parents, that the state regulate intercourse and conception, Simon feels that "here we have the most dramatic kind of confirmation of an unconscious primal scene fantasy 'ordered regulated intercourse,' not 'in the dark' is the aim and, as far as possible, intercourse should be dissociated from biological and social parenthood" (p. 177). Finally, Simon concludes that the allegory of the cave with its contrast between light and darkness, the plight of the prisoners when they enter the world of sunlight and realize they had been living in a world of illusion, has its parallel in the child's experience of "the darkness of the bedroom, seeing the shadows and hearing the echoes of parental intercourse.

In Socrates' famous dictum "the unexamined life is not worth living »
and with the development of the Socratic method, Lear (6) feels we have
the ancestor of the psychoanalytic method:

> After all, he fashioned a method of cross-examination, designed to
> elicit conflicts which had hitherto remained unconscious inside the
> interlocutor. Like the cathartic method, this inquiry was meant to
> be therapeutic. His was not a abstract inquiry into, say the nature
> of piety, but a practical attempt to help the "analysand" live a better
> life. For Socrates, "How shall I live?" is the fundamental question
> confronting each person; his peculiar form of examination was
> intended to help a person to answer it well. That is why Socrates
> had his own fundamental rule: state only what you believe. The
> "analysand" was not allowed to try out a debating position, but had
> to bring his own commitments to the inquiry. If the inquiry led to
> contradiction, it was not reductio of an abstract position with no
> putative owner, but of the "analysand's" own commitments. That is
> also why Socrates, like a contemporary psychoanalyst, disavowed
> knowledge of how the "analysand" should answer the fundamental
> question. The point of Socratic examination was to help people to
> be able to ask and answer the question for themselves. (p. 56–57)

Lear observes that the dictum was among the last words Socrates voiced at
his trial for both heresy and corrupting youth. Since he was found guilty
and sentenced to death, Lear, somewhat mordantly, suggests that in this
instance the Socratic method was "a psychotherapeutic disaster." As Lear
notes, Socrates' "cross-examination was meant to make people better, but it
provoked the demos to act out its murderous impulses." This is the crucial
point of departure for the psychoanalytic method and the Socratic dialogue.

In psychoanalysis, the emotions and their primeval instinctual roots are at the center of the dialogue, especially in the cauldron of the transference, whereas in the Socratic dialogue there exists an ill-founded belief that rational thought will transcend the irrational. Perhaps this countervailing belief in rationality arose because of the ubiquity of the irrational in Greek culture (see Dodds below). In his ideal republic, Plato would abolish those visceral esthetic elements that pander, in his opinion, to irrational emotionality, such as music and poetry, but, as we unfortunately well know from the horrific history of the 20th century, the primitive irrational elements of the individual and collective psyche are always ready to erupt into action. Only through acknowledging and addressing their omnipresence can we have any hope of containing them. This understanding is the great contribution of psychoanalysis to the human condition.

There always exists the reductionistic danger of making an isomorphic connection between the thought of ancient Greece and that of our own day. This is parallel to the adultomorphic fallacy in psychoanalysis—that of assuming we understand the childhood world of a patient based on our knowledge of their adult thoughts and fantasies or that the mental life of the child can be reconstructed from our analysis of an adult and the residues of his or her infantile neurosis. The mental world of 5th to 3rd century B.C.E. Greece was radically different, even alien, from ours as the great scholar E.R. Dodds has brilliantly demonstrated in his work *The Greeks and the Irrational* (7). He shows that Euripides' horrifying description in The Bacchae wherein Pentheus is torn apart by the maenads who are in a state of ecstatic exaltation is "not to be accounted for in terms of "the imagination alone"; that inscriptional evidence reveals a closer relationship with actual cult than Victorian scholars realized; and that the maenad however mythical certain of her acts, is not in essence a mythological character, but an observed human type" (p. 278). Dodds quotes Diodorus:

in many Greek states congregations of women assemble every second year and the unmarried girls are allowed to carry the thyrsus and share the transports of the elders." Thus Dodds concludes "this strange rite described in The Bacchae and practiced by women's societies at Delphi was certainly practiced elsewhere also. " And further: "there must have been a time when the maenads really became for a few hours or days what their name implies—wild women whose human personality has been temporarily replaced by another" (p. 271) and "that there once existed a more potent, because more dreadful form of this sacrament, viz., the rending and perhaps the eating of food in the shape of men; and that the story of Pentheus is in part a reflection of that act" (p. 278).

This speaks to an important aspect of ancient Greek society that has parallels not with the religious practices of the modern West, but with esoteric religious practices that are the domain of the cultural anthropologist, e.g., Voodoo in Haiti and Santeria and its equivalents in the Caribbean and Bahia. Dodds examines Homeric thought and concludes: "To ask whether Homer's people are determinists or libertarians is a fantastic anachronism: the question has never occurred to them, and if it were put to them it would be very difficult to make them understand what it meant" (p. 7). Dodds notes, with regard to "a people so civilized, clear-headed and rational as the Ionians (Homer's Greeks)" that "I doubt if the early literature of any other European people—even my own superstitious countrymen, the Irish—postulates supernatural interference in human behavior with such frequency or over so wide a field" (p. 13). Socrates in Phaedrus states that "our greatest blessings come to us by way of madness." He went on, as Dodds observes, to distinguish four types of "divine madness" which are produced "by a divinely wrought change in our customary social norms." Dionysian madness of the ecstatic bacchanal was to satisfy and relieve the impulse to reject responsibility" an essentially cathartic phenomenon whereby repressed irrational conflicts could be relieved in a ritual outlet. Dodd's remarkable analysis of Greek culture through a close reading of its extant literature and his own sophisticated cultural anthropological understanding demonstrates quite clearly that classical Greek society was far removed from ours. Nonetheless the anlage of many of our most cherished "rationalist" ideas are to be found in this antique world so permeated with magical and "irrational" beliefs.

The truly original Greek ancestor of the psychoanalytic enterprise was to be found well before Socrates and Plato. It was the inscription on the Temple of Apollo at Delphi, the home of the Pythia, the prestigious divine oracle who became possessed by the god and spoke his words directly. (Another example, as Dodds points out, of the power of the irrational in ancient Greek society). The inscription read "Know Thyself" Socrates advanced this admonition with his declaration: "Knowledge is virtue." The radical revolution of 18th century Romanticism, as Berlin (8) has explicated, undermined this central pillar of western culture: "It seems to me, first, that certain among the romantics cut the deepest of all the roots of the classical outlook ... namely, the belief that values, the answers to questions of action and choice, could be discovered at all . and maintained there were no answers to some of these questions, either subjective empirical or a priori." And further: "Thirdly, my thesis is that by their positive doctrine the romantics introduced a new set of values, not reconcilable with the old, and that most Europeans are today the heirs of both opposing traditions. We accept both outlooks, and shift from one foot to the other in a fashion that we cannot avoid if we are honest with ourselves, but which is not intellectually coherent" (p. 175).

As I have suggested elsewhere (10), this Romantic thesis provided the forum for object relations theory in psychoanalysis through its emphasis on individual subjectivity, the centrality of emotional experience and the potential transmuting power of the relationship between self and object. Object relations theory has its intellectual roots in Romanticism and not, as Lear would suggest, in Plato's delineation of the individual psyche's relation to the polis. Nonetheless, the classical ego-psychological model of psychoanalysis, like so much of our intellectual worldview has its origins in the extraordinary innovations and advances in human thought that the ancient Greeks wrought. The therapeutic power of psychoanalysis and psychodynamic psychotherapy based on the healing power of both the word and the therapeutic relationship was eloquently anticipated in Plato's Charmides (11):

If the head and body are to be well, you must begin by curing the soul— that is the first essential thing. And the cure of the soul, my dear youth, has to be effected by the use of certain charms, and these charms are fair words, and by them temperance is implanted in the soul, and where temperance comes and stays, then health is speedily imparted, not only to the head but to the whole body. (p. 181)

REFERENCES

1. Plato. *The republic*, Book IX, pp. 334–335, Loeb Classical Library, Harvard University Press, 1987; B. Simon (Transl.) in Journal of the History of the Behavioral Sciences, 8, 43, 1972.
2. Plato. *Phaedrus*, Vol. 1, pp. 233–285, B. Jowett (Transl.). New York: Random House, 1937.
3. Freud S (1923). The ego and the id. *Standard Edition*, Vol. 19. London: Hogarth Press, 1961.
4. Simon B (1978). *Mind and madness in ancient Greece*. Ithaca & London: Cornell University Press.

5. Hippocrates. *The sacred disease.* In F. Adams (Ed.). The genuine works of Hippocrates. New York: William wood, 1929.

6. Lear J (1998). *Open minded. Working out the logic of the soul.* Cambridge and London: Harvard University Press.

7. Dodds ER (1971). *The Greeks and the irrational.* Berkeley, CA: University of California Press.

8. Berlin I (1997). *The sense of reality.* New York: Farrar, Straus & Giroux.

9. Buckley P (1997). Psychoanalysis and its romantic rebellion. *Journal of the American Psychoanalytic Association,* 45, 577–587.

10. Plato. Charmides. In D. Watt (Transl.). *Early Socratic dialogues.* London, New York: Penguin Books, 1987.

CHAPTER 9

Psychoanalysis and its Romantic Rebellion

What then does the poet? He considers man and the objects that
surround him as acting and reacting upon each other, so as to produce
an infinite complexity of pain and pleasure.
—*William Wordsworth*

Two centuries ago, Western culture underwent a revolutionary transformation at the hands of what came to be called the romantic movement. Reacting against classicism and the Enlightenment with its emphasis on rationality, order, and inevitable social progress, romanticism promoted the primacy of subjectivity, unfettered imagination, and emotional spontaneity. In the realm of music, romanticism has been viewed as an art that emphasizes the subjective and emotional possibilities and neglects the formal and structural point of view. William Wordsworth, the standard-bearer of romanticism in English literature, extolled "the spontaneous overflow of powerful feelings" and the wedding of the mind to the outside world, while the art historian Kenneth Clark has seen romanticism as "a rebellion against static authority."

Of late we have witnessed a revolutionary movement within psychoanalytic theory and practice. Various rubrics have been assigned to aspects of this phenomenon: object relations theory, self psychology, intersubjectivity, and, lately, relational psychoanalysis. While some commentators (Cooper 1987) have placed this movement within the framework of contemporary cultural currents such as postmodernism,the philosophical ascendancy of synchrony (things as they are, ignoring how they have become that way) and hermeneutics, I would suggest that we have been witnessing a late flowering of the romantic movement in which the new theoretical stance emphasizes individual subjectivity, the centrality of emotional experience, "Wordsworthian" relationships between self and object, and the transmuting power of the therapeutic relationship, all in contrast to the classical structural model of ego psychology.

An example of the relationship between romanticism and some of the issues that presently preoccupy psychoanalysis is provided by Turner (1988) in his perceptive study of the cultural origins of Winnicott's concern with creativity and play. He convincingly shows the affinity between Winnicott's concepts and Wordsworth's understanding of poetry. Turner posits that in Wordsworth's *Prelude* of 1798–1799 is to be found a developed version of object relations psychology based on a relational interplay between mind and nature whereby Wordsworth explored the culture of subjectivity. Turner observes that "Wordsworth described the mysterious wedding of the human mind to the visible universe as the 'great consummation' to which all his poetry was to be the 'spousal verse'; his sense of the relational drew him to what might be created between subject and object, an area for which he had no language and which he sought to articulate by means of metaphor" (p. 489). Within psychoanalysis, this sense of the relational was to find its fullest expression in W.R.D. Fairbairn's declaration (1952) that "psychology is a study of the relationships of the individual to his objects, whilst, in similar terms, psychopathology may be said to resolve itself more specifically into a study of the relationship of the ego to its internalized objects" (p. 60).

Akin to Fairbairn, modern relational psychoanalysis holds technical views radically different from classical views on such fundamental issues as resistance, the management of transference, and the cause of therapeutic change. These perspectives stem from Fairbairn's manifesto as to the "true" nature of psychology and psychopathology, one that is uncompromisingly environmentalist in posture and committed to the interactional use of the therapeutic relationship as the primary agent of psychological change. For Fairbairn, the greatest source of resistance is "fear of the release of bad objects from the unconscious for, when such bad objects are released, the world around the patient becomes peopled with devils which are too terrifying for him to face" and in order to dissolve the bonds to these previously indispensable bad objects it is necessary that "the analyst present himself as a good object to the patient in reality" and further that "all situations should be interpreted, not in terms of gratification, but in terms of object-relationships (including, of course, relationships with internalized objects)" (p. 74). Here we are firmly in the arena of Wordsworthian relational interplay.

The books under review in this essay are all examples of the application of relational concepts to psychoanalysis, concepts that are central to the present theoretical controversies that pervade the field: one-person versus two-person psychologies; the intrapsychic versus the interpersonal and its corollary, unconscious conflict versus external trauma; and interpretive insight versus therapeutic experience. Such dichotomies, of course, are often only useful for polemical purposes, but they do have the virtue of sharpening debate, challenging orthodoxy, and furthering our understanding of the nature of the psychoanalytic situation.

FROM INSTINCT TO SELF: SELECTED PAPERS OF W.R.D. FAIRBAIRN. VOL. I: CLINICAL AND THEORETICAL PAPERS. Edited by *David E Scharff* and *Ellinor Fairbairn Birtles*, 172 pp. VOL. II: APPLICATIONS AND EARLY CONTRIBUTIONS. Edited by *Ellinor Fairbairn Birtles* and *David E. Scharff*, 490 pp. Northvale, NJ: Aronson, 1994.

While there had been intimations of the importance of relational considerations in Freud's clinical theory and in the writings of Ferenczi and Rank (Fogel 1993), it was Fairbairn's clarion call—"the object and not gratification is the ultimate aim of libidinal striving"—that initiated this most radical departure from classical theory. Living in Scotland in relative isolation from the centers of analytic activity, Fairbairn produced a series of papers, beginning in the 1940s, that limned an object relations model of developmental psychology and pathogenesis. His major papers were published together in *Psychoanalytic Studies of the Personality* (1952), and subsequently his ideas were disseminated by two of his students and analysands, John D. Sutherland and Harry Guntrip.

It is only within the last fifteen years, however, that a true awareness has arisen of how central Fairbairn's concepts are to the current theoretical ferment in psychoanalysis, most notably to the creation of relational psychoanalysis. Otto Kernberg, James S. Grotstein, and Stephen Mitchell in particular, through their acknowledgment of his influence on their own thinking, have been key figures in effecting this recognition of Fairbairn's intellectual stature and his importance in the evolution of psychoanalytic thought. David E. Scharff and Fairbairn's daughter, Ellinor Fairbairn Birtles, have compiled, in Volume I, those papers of Fairbairn that were published after the appearance in 1952 of *Psychoanalytic Studies of the Personality,* while in Volume II they have collected his early letters and unpublished papers dating from 1927 to 1937. Given the extensive compass of modern clinical work and theory foreshadowed by Fairbairn's formulations, the editors have performed an invaluable service that will greatly enhance future scholarship (though whether Fairbairn himself, given his retiring nature, would have countenanced the publication of virtually everything he wrote before and after the papers collected in *Psychoanalytic Studies of the Personality,* is perhaps moot).

The philosophical origins of one of Fairbairn's more controversial postulates, namely that normal human relationships are fundamentally interpersonal and not, like their pathological equivalents, internalized, are illuminated by the editors, who draw attention to the importance of Fairbairn's rigorous training in philosophy and of the influence of Hegel's *Science of Logic* on his thinking. They note that Hegel's text "is a close examination of the relationship of subject to object" and further that "Hegel sees desire as essentially unsatisfying; where dissatisfaction leads to the need to control the object and, hence, the need to transform and own that object" (vol. 1, p. xiv). Since, as they observe, it was Hegel "who saw each individual's participation with others as the vehicle for development towards full human personality, ... this process [being] inseparably connected to the experience of subject-object relationships" (vol. 1, p. xvii), their assertion that it was from Hegel that Fairbairn drew the beginnings of inspiration for his theory of the personality has much merit and places Fairbairn's theories firmly within the tradition of the continental European philosophy of idealism in which he was so well versed, one that had strong affinities with the romantic movement.

The republication here of one of Fairbairn's late papers, "The Nature of Hysterical States" (1954), is especially valuable, as it provides a comprehensive summation of his model of the inner object world (which he referred to as the basic endopsychic situation) and uses more detailed clinical data to substantiate his thesis than is typical of his writing. Fairbairn's doctoral submission of 1929 (published here for the first time) is titled "The Relationship of Dissociation and Repression Considered from the Viewpoint of Medical Psychology." A closely reasoned scholarly treatise, it represents, as the editors observe, "a milestone on the road to his later work on the centrality of splitting and repression in the organization of the personality" (vol. 2, p. 7). In his mature work, of which "The Nature of Hysterical States" is the exemplar, Fairbairn saw splitting and repression as the mechanisms that lead to internal unconscious self and object structures in dynamic affective relationship with one another (a structural concept later adopted by Kernberg). In this paper, Fairbairn adumbrates a view of conversion symptoms radically different from that of Freud, namely, the use of the body for the control of internal object relations. He further posits that "the resistance of the hysterical patient is not so much a resistance to the psychotherapeutic process as a resistance to the psychotherapist himself" (vol. 1, p. 14).

A great strength of these volumes lies in the editors' lucid and insightful commentaries on the relevance of each of Fairbairn's writings and lectures to the unfolding evolution of his work, culminating in his almost mathematical two-page synopsis of 1963, "An Object Relations Theory of the Personality." Scharff and Birtles demonstrate how rigorous and far-reaching was Fairbairn's reasoning, and thanks to their efforts the reader is provided entrée into a subtle mind at work, one profoundly influenced by the dialectic of Hegel, engaged in an heroic struggle to divine and map the unconscious mind. This is the intellectual journey. The more hidden, private, and emotion-ridden elements of that journey are to be found in Sutherland's remarkable biography of Fairbairn (1989). There the much neglected issues of the influence of personal history, subjective experience, and individual conflicts on the origins of psychoanalytic ideas are laid bare in Fairbairn's case, and the psychodynamic provenance of his romantic rebellion against classical theory can be more fully comprehended.

PERSONAL RELATIONS THERAPY: THE COLLECTED PAPERS OF H.J.S. GUNTRIP. Edited by *Jeremy Hazell*. Northvale, NJ: Aronson, 1994, 232 pp., $35.00.

Aptly, Jeremy Hazell's edition of Harry Guntrip's papers begins with a quotation from Wordsworth's "Intimations of Immortality from

Recollections of Early Childhood," a stanza that captures the nature of Guntrip's personal and professional quest. Hazell sets the papers in the context of Guntrip's search for self-understanding and persuasively argues that his theory always closely followed his subjective experience.

Prior to becoming a psychotherapist, Guntrip was a Congregational minister, and during this period of his life he experienced severe states of "exhaustion" whenever he was obliged to be in his mother's presence. Following a classical analysis that did little to relieve his symptoms, Guntrip began a training analysis with Fairbairn. In a personal communication to Hazell, he wrote: "Fairbairn saved the situation for me as a psychotherapist ... [for] without that deeper knowledge I could not have gone on" (p. 5). Nonetheless, this analysis came to an end through a combination of Fairbairn's failing health and Guntrip's feeling that many of his neurotic issues remained unresolved. At this juncture, Guntrip had become convinced of the utility of therapeutic regression both for himself and for his patients. In a 1960 paper he wrote, "Psychotherapy ... is really an invitation into an open system in touch with outer reality, an opportunity to grow out of deep-down fears in a good-object relationship with the therapist. But this will only succeed in a radical way if the therapist can reach the profoundly withdrawn Regressed Ego, relieve its fears and start it on the road to regrowth and rebirth ..." (p. 155). Aware that this was consonant with Winnicott's views, he began treatment with him in the 1960s. Guntrip's account of his therapies is one of the more remarkable experiential works to be found in the psychoanalytic literature; there he states that he found Fairbairn to be more orthodox (i.e., classical) in practice than in theory, while Winnicott was more revolutionary in practice than in theory.

A prolific and fluent writer, as this book makes clear, Guntrip was instrumental in bringing Fairbairn's work to a wider audience while making original contributions and elaborating Fairbairn's ideas. As Greenberg and Mitchell (1983) have pointed out, however, he parted drastically from

Fairbairn by claiming that the regressed ego constitutes the core of all psychopathology and that the central dynamic thrust, in contradistinction to Fairbairn, is withdrawal from objects. The personal origins of this idea are to be found in his account of his treatment with Winnicott, who observed, "In some sense a part of you did die. You had an experience of death, and need to find out that there is a way out with me, from having to be one of mother's dead objects" (p. 19).

Guntrip is a vivid example of the "wounded healer" so familiar to anthropologists who have studied the life histories of shamans in other cultures. When he wrote that "real psychotherapy does as much for the therapist as for the patient," he was revealing a truth not often faced (Guntrip 1968, p. 354).

OBJECT RELATIONS THERAPY OF PHYSICAL AND SEXUAL TRAUMA. By *Jill Savege Scharff* and *David E. Scharff*. Northvale, NJ: Aronson, 1994, 392 pp., $47.50.

As Jill and David Scharff confess, little is more emotionally taxing for the psychoanalytic clinician than the treatment of the survivor of abuse: "As writers, we procrastinated, studied everything else, and wrote other books first, because recording our countertransference reawakened the memory of our reception of the patient's trauma. As therapists, and then as writers, we have felt nauseated, anguished, frightened, guilty and helpless" (p. xvi). The authors call attention to their private subjective concerns about "exhibitionism, betrayal, breaking of boundaries, exploitation of the patient and traumatizing the reader" and have produced a work rich in clinical detail that is at times horrifying because of their patients' hellish experiences (p. xvi).

For four years in the 1930s, Fairbairn worked in a clinic devoted to the treatment of children and adolescents; in 1935, he published a remarkably candid and progressive assessment, for the times, on the ubiquity of child abuse (reprinted in Volume II of *From Instinct to Self*). This clinical experience, as the Scharffs suggest, was of considerable import to the later development of his object relations theory, which for them has the greatest explanatory power for understanding and treating the abused patient. Fairbairn's work with abused children was undoubtedly key to his view that the more unsatisfying (and traumatizing) an object is in reality, the more the child is forced to internalize it in order to both deny and control its real and imagined malevolence. Fairbairn (1952) expressed this concept poetically when he wrote, "It is better to be a sinner in a world ruled by God than to live in a world ruled by the Devil" (p. 66). Similarly, Fairbairn's mechanism of splitting and repression is seen by the authors as the cause of the splits in the self regularly found in the survivors of abuse, taking its most extreme form in multiple personality disorders.

Inevitably, the authors engage the fantasy versus reality of trauma, the repressed memory debate that has reached such a cacophonous pitch of late, a controversy that pits fantasy against reality as explanations of trauma. This subject is beyond the scope of this essay, but, suffice it to say, they promulgate a measured approach to this issue that fits with that recently articulated by Simon (1992).

The strength of this work lies in the wealth of detailed clinical material that the authors provide, including examples of cases that failed. While listening to one of his patients, David Scharff has the feeling of being transfixed by the dreadful tale like the listener in Coleridge's *Rime of the Ancient Mariner:* "He held him with his glittering eye— / The Wedding Guest stood still, / And listens like a three years' child: / The Mariner hath his will." The reader of this book will often have this experience.

CLOSE ENCOUNTERS: A RELATIONAL VIEW OF THE THERAPEUTIC PROCESS. By *Robert Winer.* Northvale, NJ: Aronson, 1994, 296 pp., $35.00.

In Robert Winer's book we find the personal intellectual and emotional odyssey of a psychotherapist. Winer exposes his struggles with clinical work, with theory and his own professional evolution. He states that "the therapist, like the artist, must invent himself" (p. 10), a credo that would have found favor with the romantics. He is refreshingly candid about his eclectic endeavors to create a workable theoretical synthesis for his clinical work. Ultimately, this is a relational model, one in which the clinical situation is a "complex field in which both parties are thinking and reacting, and where the flow of influence is Byzantine. Each will influence the other with his ideas, his moods, his transferences, his countertransferences, his character style. Their shared gravitational field will draw certain issues in and spin others off. Both participants are wrestling with themselves and acting upon each other in ways that are both within and beyond their ken" (p. 9).

Winer acknowledges his debt to Loewald (1979), who suggests that we are less individual than we realize. Are we, he asks, "justified in simply equating the psychic life with the intrapsychic?" (p. 399). Loewald (1960), in his innovative paper "On the Therapeutic Action of Psychoanalysis," posited that therapeutic effects are a result of ego development resuming in therapy as a consequence of the relationship with a new object. This ego development, in his view, is due to the internalization of an interaction process between patient and therapist, a position not too dissimilar from that of Kohut, another of Winer's prime influences.

Winer, through his self-revelations, engages the reader in a dialectical encounter somewhat similar to that he proposes as the essence of therapy. Such provocative (and romantic) statements as "For at the heart of the therapeutic process, in those therapies where both parties are truly engaged, we find cycles of collusion and extrication, corruption and redemption" evoke an emotional response (Winer, p. 254). In the end there is something very appealing about the writer, a consequence of his willingness to confront the demons and perils of therapeutic work. Appropriately, he finishes his text by recounting and analyzing one of his own dreams, at the end of which he comments, "Writing, treating and supervising at their best are all quickenings, breathing life, sowing seeds, discovering fire" (p. 259), suggesting that, for Robert Winer in these endeavors, an identification with the romantic hero Prometheus is close at hand.

DISCUSSION

Mitchell (1988) has been the leading modern advocate of a purely relational model for psychoanalysis, one in which drive theory is abandoned completely and conflict derives entirely from relationships with others. Bachant, Lynch, and Richards (1995) have trenchantly [585] criticized this as an extremist position that oversimplifies key aspects of Freud's theoretical system. They target in particular Mitchell's insistence on offering Freud's tension reduction, drive discharge model as Freudian theory. They observe that this model bears little relation to the contemporary classical view of drive as part of unconscious fantasies that organize childhood memory and experience and the drive component as part of a broader theory of the dynamic unconscious. They believe that in relational theory there is a drastic shift away from the importance of the dynamic unconscious to a focus on the interaction between patient and analyst, a move to a two-person psychology and away from intrapsychic conflict, leading to an impoverishment of understanding of what really motivates behavior and determines symptoms and the form of transference.

The books under review here do not support their contention that the relational perspective adversely affects the psychoanalytic situation by interfering with *true* understanding of the patient. They are more correct when they contend that there is a place for both constructivistic and positivistic epistemological perspectives in psychoanalysis in order to make some degree of sense out of the complexity of the clinical situation. It is of interest in this regard that while Fairbairn was quite categorical in his view that the development of the individual hinges on the vicissitudes of object relationships and not on the vicissitudes of the drives, a drive concept with its attendant unconscious fantasies was not really abandoned. As Eagle (1984) has observed, in Fairbairn's theory object seeking is as primary and as intrinsically biological as are the sexual and aggressive drives in classical theory.

William Blake's exhortation and rebuke, "If the doors of perception were cleansed every thing would appear to man as it is, infinite. / For man has closed himself up, till he sees all things thro' narrow chinks of his cavern," was embraced by the romantic movement that proceeded to expand our vision of the relational interplay of the self and the surrounding world through its emphasis on subjectivity. Kohut's assertion (1959) that "the limits of psychoanalysis are … defined by the potential limits of introspection and empathy" is a further manifestation of this culture of subjectivity within modern psychoanalytic thinking (p. 482). For all its radical nature, the romantic movement could not have existed without the classicism that preceded it, and while romanticism arose in reaction to the orthodoxy of the past, it also sprang from it. The dangers of unbridled romanticism lie in the worship of ungovernable forces and mystical exaltation in communion with the other, elements to be found in both Byron and Wordsworth. The classical tradition in psychoanalysis, as in art, provides a welcome antidote to these propensities. As Clark (1973), in his study of romantic painters, observes, "classicism and romanticism in artists of the first rank always coexist and overlap" (p. 12). Freud, a classicist par excellence, was not averse to the insights of romanticism. In a letter to Jung he wrote, "It would not have escaped you that our cures come about through attaching the libido reigning in the unconscious…. Where this fails the patient will not make the effort or else does not listen when we translate his material to him. It is in essence a cure through love" (Freud and Jung 1974, pp. 12–13).

REFERENCES

Bachant, J.L, Lynch, A.A., & Richards, A.D. (1995). Relational models in psychoanalytic theory. *Psychoanalytic Psychology* 12:71–87.

Clark, K. (1973). *The Romantic Rebellion.* New York: Harper & Row.

Cooper, A.M. (1987). Changes in psychoanalytic ideas: Transference interpretation. *Journal of the American Psychoanalytic Association* 35:77–98.

Eagle, M.N. (1984). *Recent Developments in Psychoanalysis.* New York: McGraw-Hill.

Fairbairn, W.R.D. (1952). *An Object-Relations Theory of the Personality.* New York: Basic Books.

Freud, S., & Jung, C.G. (1974). *The Freud-Jung Letters,* ed. W. McGuire, transl. Ralph Manheim & R.F.C. Hall. Princeton, NJ: Princeton University Press.

Fogel, G.I. (1993). A transitional phase in our understanding of the psychoanalytic process: A new look at Ferenczi and Rank. *Journal of the American Psychoanalytic Association* 41:585–602.

Greenberg, J., & Mitchell, S. (1983). *Object Relations in Psychoanalytic Theory.* Cambridge: Harvard University Press.

Guntrip, H.J.S. (1968). *Schizoid Phenomena, Object Relations and the Self.* London: Hogarth.

Kohut, H. (1959). Introspection, empathy and psychoanalysis. *Journal of the American Psychoanalytic Association* 7:459–483.

Loewald, H. (1960). On the therapeutic action of psychoanalysis. *International Journal of Psycho-Analysis* 41:16–33.

———— (1979). The waning of the oedipus complex. In *Papers on Psychoanalysis*. New Haven: Yale University Press, 1980.

Mitchell, S. (1988). *Relational Concepts in Psychoanalysis: An Integration*. Cambridge: Harvard University Press.

Simon, B. (1992). "Incest—see under oedipus complex": The history of an error in psychoanalysis. *Journal of the American Psychoanalytic Association* 40:955–988.

Sutherland, J.D. (1989). *Fairbairn's Journey into the Interior*. London: Free Association Books.

Turner, J. (1988). Wordsworth and Winnicott in the area of play. *International Review of Psycho-Analysis* 15:481–497.

CHAPTER 10

Revolution and Evolution: A Brief Intellectual History of American Psychoanalysis during the Past Two Decades

The past twenty years have witnessed revolutionary changes in the theory and practice of psychoanalysis in the United States. The previously dominant clinical model of ego psychology with its emphasis on ubiquitous unconscious conflict between instinctual drives and the demands of reality and conscience, all mediated by the ego, is now but one of an array of differing theoretical views vying for attention. The alternative competing theoretical and clinical domains can be loosely categorized under the rubrics of object relations, self psychology, and the off-shoots of these which include the relational and intersubjective frames. These insurgent models of mental functioning and development, all of which grow out of object relations theory and thus overlap conceptually, have significant implications for psychoanalytic technique.

It is the purpose of this article to review aspects of these models and the historic and revolutionary changes that their appearance have effected in the psychoanalytic landscape. A brief summary will also be made of the more evolutionary advances that have occurred in ego psychology during the past two decades. The extant literature on these issues is complex and voluminous, not to say vast. In advance, I apologize for the necessarily selective and even idiosyncratic nature of this paper. Inevitably, many original and important contributions to the evolving mosaic that makes up contemporary psychoanalysis are ignored or short-changed.

SELF PSYCHOLOGY

'Love seeketh only Self to please,
To bind another to its delight,
Joys in another's loss of ease,
And builds a Hell in Heaven's despite'
Blake

The advent of Heinz Kohut's 1971 monograph, *The Analysis of the Self* (I), marks the beginning of the revolutionary movement in American psychoanalysis. Kohut's clinical work with narcissistic disturbances led him to postulate a separate narcissistic line of development occurring alongside psychosexual and ego development. As his theory evolved, he developed a complete self psychology and abandoned concepts of instinctual drives as primary (2). Kohut's view, like earlier object relations theorists, most notably Fairbairn (3), is an environmentalist one which posits that early and pervasive empathic failures on the part of parents or their surrogates leads to what he termed *self-object failures* and developmental arrests. Psychopathology is no longer viewed as a manifestation of inadequately resolved conflict as it is in the ego psychology model, but as a reflection of deficits in development that result in defective internal self-structures.

In a remarkable clinical paper "The Two Analyses of Mr. Z" (4), Kohut contrasted his use of the "classical" conflict model in his treatment of a male patient with the subsequent utilization of the self-psychology deficit model in the patient's second analysis. In the first analysis Kohut notes:

The centre of the analytic stage was—occupied—by transference phenomena and memories concerning his, as I then saw it, pathogenic conflicts in the area of infantile sexuality and

168

aggression—his Oedipus complex, his castration anxiety, his childhood masturbation, his fantasy of the phallic woman, and especially, his preoccupation with the primal scene, (p. 5)

Kohut's initial approach to the patient's narcissistic disturbances manifest in grandiosity and narcissistic demands was that

[they] were worked through, both in so far as they were the continuation of his fixation on the pre-oedipal mother and in so far as they were clung to as a defense against oedipal competitiveness and castration fear. (p. 8)

Pleased with the clinical work he had conducted, Kohut felt that,

everything seemed to have fallen into place. We had reached the oedipal conflict, the formerly unconscious ambivalence toward the oedipal father had come to the fore, there were the expected attempts at regressive evasion and temporary exacerbations of pre-oedipal conflict and there was ultimately a period of anticipatory mourning for the analyst and the relationship with him—It all seemed right, (p. 9)

Four and a half years after the termination of the first analysis, Mr. Z returned to analysis. Kohut observed:

that the first analysis had not achieved a cure of his masochistic propensities via structural change, but that they had only become suppressed and had now shifted to his work and to his life in general, (p. 10)

Kohut became aware of something that he had not entertained during the first analysis, that his patient was establishing an idealizing transference. On this occasion, Kohut allowed an unfolding of the patient's idealization of him. Gradually this became replaced by a mirror-transference of the merger-type.

> The glow of well-being and inner security that he experienced in consequence of feeling himself within the milieu provided by the idealized analyst faded away, and in its stead the patient became self-centered, demanding, insisting on perfect empathy, and inclined to react with rage at the slightest out-of-tuneness with his psychological states, (p. 11)

This time, Kohut did not regard this phenomenon as defensive but saw it as a revival of the patient's early childhood experience with his mother. Now Kohut viewed the patient's self in the transference "as desperately— and often hopelessly—struggling to disentangle itself from the noxious maternal self-object" (p. 12). Painstakingly, Kohut provided himself as a "good object" so that "the analyst-father was experienced as strong and masculine, and so did the analysand-son now experience himself," developing an independent self free from his enslavement to the maternal self-object. As Kohut noted in this second analysis the patient's most significant psychological achievement was the breaking of the deep merger ties with his mother.

While Kohut did not abandon interpretation, he had now, however, developed a radically different technical approach from the classical ego-psychological model, one in which he gave pre-eminence to the curative power of the empathic therapeutic relationship. For instance, he stated that the "active encouragement of idealization is not desirable... But a spontaneously occurring therapeutic mobilization of the idealized parent image or of the grandiose self is indeed to be welcomed and must not be interfered with."

He further commented:

> if the analyst's interpretations are non-condemnatory; if he can clarify to the patient in concrete terms... that these archaic attitudes are comprehensible, adaptive and valuable within the context of the total state of personality development of which they form a part... then the mature segment of the ego will not turn away from the grandiosity of the archaic self or from the awesome features of the overestimated, narcissistically experienced object. Over and over again, in small, psychologically manageable portions, the ego will deal with the disappointment at having to recognize that the claims of the grandiose self are unrealistic.... And over and over again, in small psychologically manageable portions, the ego will deal with the disappointment of having to recognize that the idealized object is unavailable or imperfect. And, in response to this experience, it will withdraw a part of idealizing investment from the object and strengthen the corresponding internal structures. (1, p. 229)

Working in Scotland in the 1940s, Fairbairn anticipated this theory of therapeutic change promulgated by Kohut when he wrote:

> It follows from what precedes that the ruling aims of analytical technique should be: 1. to enable the patient to release from his unconscious "buried" bad objects which have been internalized because originally they seemed indispensable, and which have been repressed because originally they seemed intolerable, and 2. to promote a dissolution of the libidinal bonds whereby the patient is attached to these hitherto indispensable bad objects. The fulfillment

of the second of these aims will follow more or less automatically (if somewhat tardily) from the first, provided that a satisfactory transference situation has been established and that the analyst presents himself as a good object to the patient in reality. For the fulfillment of the first of these aims a satisfactory transference situation is also indispensable. Otherwise the patient will never acquire a sufficient sense of security to enable him to risk a release of his buried bad objects. (3, p. 74)

A full and insightful explication and commentary on the seminal theoretical work of Fairbairn is to be found in the volume edited by Grotstein & Rinsley (5) that underlines the crucial importance of this Scottish pioneer to the current ferment in American psychoanalysis.

SELF PSYCHOLOGY SINCE KOHUT AND THE RISE OF INTERSUBJECTIVITY

In an essay entitled "Self Psychology after Kohut: One Theory or Many" (6), Morton & Estelle Shane contend that six basic attributes can be seen to define contemporary self-psychology. They observe that three of these are attributes delineated by Stolorow and his collaborators (7), namely:

the unwavering application of the empathic-introspective mode as defining and limiting the domain of inquiry; the primacy of self experience; and the concepts of the lifelong need for self object function and the varieties of self object transference, (p. 779)

Shane & Shane add to this list:

the emphasis on attachment as the central motivation for the self, in the broad sense, in its effort to establish and maintain self-cohesiveness; the concept of aggression as reactive to frustration; and the emphasis on the psychoanalytic process as carrying with it, along with insight, a significant developmental power and thrust, (p. 779)

Shane and Shane note that Stolorow and his coworkers concluded that

psychoanalysis is the science of the intersubjective, focused on the interplay between the two differently organized subjective worlds of patient and analyst—pathology itself becomes understood as a kind of two-person event, a function of both patient and analyst. Patients do not come into treatment with specific self-object needs and specific self pathology... but how these needs are met and responded to in the intersubjective psychoanalytic field can significantly influence the severity of this pathology as well as the course and outcome of treatment. In a real way—every diagnosis and every course of treatment can only be comprehended in the field comprised of the two individual subjectivities in interaction with one another, joined together by an exclusive intersubjective empathic-introspective stance, (p. 780)

Thus, Stolorow and his group expanded Kohut's original delineation of the margins of psychoanalysis as "defined by the potential limits of introspection and empathy" on the part of the analyst. In essence they brought a constructivist view of the psychoanalytic situation to the forefront some of which was anticipated by the ego psychologist Merton Gill.

Shane and Shane observe that Bacal and Newman (8) "have dedicated their efforts to bridging the gap between self psychology and object relations theories with the assumption that self psychology is in essence an object-relations theory at its core" (p. 795). They conclude that there exists not just one self psychology, but many. Goldberg (9) comments that "the continuing evolution of self-psychology has articulated with the emergence of other psychoanalytic excursions such as seen in the interpersonal and constructivist concepts"(p. 242). Goldberg states that "since self-psychology regards self objects as part of the self, it extends the concept of the person to include those others who function as part of the self" (p. 245). He avers, however, that this does not make traditional self-psychology a "two-person psychology" per se. He notes that

the crucial difference between traditional self psychology and the theory of intersubjectivity is that for the latter the transference is felt to have two basic dimensions: the self object dimension and the repetitive dimension....The essence of transference analysis lies in investigating the dimensions of transference as they take form in the ongoing intersubjective system. This system is formed by the interplay between the transference of the patient and that of the analyst. The focus is ever upon this shared construction and not upon the singular contribution of the patient projected onto the analyst, (p. 247)

Goldberg further comments that in contrast to traditional self psychology "both the branches of intersubjectivity and relational self psychology either make little use of unconscious fantasy or dispense with it altogether." Goldberg emphasizes that Kohut placed great weight on the importance of unconscious fantasy that "appeared to be the motor for ongoing growth." Inherent in this issue is an ongoing vigorous debate on the importance of the intrapsychic versus the interpersonal in the psychoanalytic situation.

174

Dunn (10) in an insightful review of intersubjectivity asserts that the concept "constitutes a major epistemological and clinical challenge to the 'classical' paradigm which is grounded in the positivist scientific orientation." He states that

> intersubjectivity embodies the notion that the very formation of the therapeutic process is derived from an inextricably intertwined mixture of the clinical participants' subjective reactions to one another. Knowledge of the patients' psychology is considered contextual and idiosyncratic to the particular clinical interaction. This interactional nexus is considered the primary force of the psychoanalytic treatment process, (p. 723)

Thus, we have a radical constructivist view of the psychoanalytic situation: "The clinician's perceptions of the patient's psychology are always shaped by the clinician's subjectivity. Conversely, the patients psychology is not conceptualized as something discoverable by an external unbiased observer" (p. 726). Dunn comments that intersubjective theorists view "the fundamental operation of mind as based in its striving for relational connections and communication, rather than discharge and gratification of instinctual pressures." Dunn, alongside many of the intersubjectivists themselves, does not acknowledge that this concept derives directly from Fairbairn who wrote: "The object, and not gratification, is the ultimate aim of libidinal striving." Jones (11) aptly summarized Fairbairn:

> If it were possible to condense Dr. Fairbairn's new ideas into one sentence it might run somewhat as follows. Instead of starting, as Freud did, from stimulation of the nervous system proceeding from excitation of various erotogenous zones and internal tensions arising from gonadic activity, Dr. Fairbairn starts at the center of

the personality, the ego, and depicts its strivings and difficulties in its endeavour to reach an object where it may find support, (p. v).

Dunn understands that the interest in, and development of, the utility of countertransference in the clinical situation was, essentially, a harbinger of the intersubjectivist movement. The focus on countertransference has led to an "interactionalist" orientation for even some adherents of the classical psychoanalytic tradition wherein the concept of enactment has achieved prominence. Dunn notes that this has been "defined, by Chused (12) as 'symbolic interactions' that begin as a patient's attempt at transference gratification, but are created by the interaction of the patient's behavior and the analysts' response" (p. 730).

RELATIONAL PSYCHOANALYSIS

What then does the poet? He considers man and the objects that surround him as acting and reacting upon each other, so as to produce an infinite complexity of pain and pleasure. "
—Wordsworth

Mitchell (13), the progenitor of Relational Psychoanalysis, takes as his premise the view that the clinical process of psychoanalysis has always been fundamentally relational. He implies that this binding concept has recently promoted what amounts to a psychoanalytic ecumenicism:

Within the major theoretical schools of analytic thought, there has been a distinct turn toward relational concepts. Contemporary Kleinian theory has been dominated by increasingly interactional versions of the concept of projective identification, which has dramatically reshaped the Kleinian vision from a purely intrapsychic model of self-contained primitive phantasies to a dense account of complex reciprocal projective and introjective influences. Contemporary self psychology has become, in major respects, increasingly relational particularly under the influence of intersubjectivity theory.... Many contemporary interpersonal analysts have moved in a relational direction, adding object relations concepts concerning internal object relations to the traditionally interpersonal account of actual transactions between people. And psychoanalytic developmental theory, across the board, has been greatly influenced by the impressive tradition of attachment theory....In the theory of clinical technique, too, relational concepts have been increasingly in evidence. The traditional classical principles of neutrality, abstinence, and anonymity, fashioned to protect the integrity of the patient as a monadic, one-person system, have generally been either abandoned or else revised into milder, less impersonal forms, emphasizing the "containing" "holding" features of the patient-analyst field....And the study of the array of patient analyst interactions linked variably with the terms "counter-transference," "enactment" and "projective identification" has become, perhaps, the dominant focus of recent articles and books on analytic technique, (p. xiv)

Mitchell acknowledges that considerable confusion exists about the relationships themselves among these different interactional concepts and lines of thought. He avers that "the variety of relational concepts pervading the recent analytic literature is best understood not as representing competing theories, but as addressing themselves to different, interwoven dimensions of relationality" (p. xv).

One of Mitchell's principal intellectual sources is Hans Loewald who had in turn studied with the German philosopher Heidegger. Heidegger's influence is to be seen in the centrality Loewald placed on language. While Loewald remained firmly in the drive theory camp (which Mitchell repudiates) Mitchell feels that for Loewald:

> Freud's language, the language of drive theory, is the archaic language (like ancient Greek for Heidegger) of psychoanalysis. It contains within itself, and evokes powerful affective resonances with both the early infantile, bodily experience it was designed to describe, (pp. 13–14).

Notwithstanding, Mitchell's attempts to view Loewald's metapsychological language as poetic, Loewald's work remains very much within the realm of ego psychology. What undoubtedly appealed to Mitchell, however, was Loewald's view of the interactive nature of the psychoanalytic situation. Loewald felt that the resumption of ego development that may take place in therapy is not simply the internalization of objects but an internalization of an interaction process between patient and therapist that includes, but is not confined to, interpretive work (14). Thus, for Mitchell

> the central feature of Loewald's revisions of Freudian theory is his shifting the locus of experience, the point of origination, from the individual to the field within which the individual comes into consciousness, and this has been making its way into contemporary Freudian thought. In the beginning, Loewald says over and over, is not the impulse; in the beginning is the field in which all individuals are embedded. Experience does not proceed, as Freud believed, from inside outward, from the id's impulse, through the ego, into negotiation with the outside world. Experience initially moves from

outside inward, from an increasingly differentiated unity of which the individual is a part to the development of the individual through an internalization of those external patterns, (p. 35).

I would like to conclude by stressing that we are at the point in thinking about complex emotions in the analytic relationship where we can move beyond polarized positions about analytic love as either real or unreal, and analytic feelings as to be either carefully restrained or loosely expressed. Love and hate within the analytic relationship are very real, but are also contextual. The asymmetrical structure of the analytic situation is a powerful shaper of the feelings that emerge within it, making certain kinds of feelings possible and precluding others. It is precisely because these feelings, as real as they are, are so context-dependent that they are not easily translatable into extra- or post-analysis relationships. And neither restraint nor expressiveness, in themselves, are useful as guides to the management of analytic feelings. Both restraint and spontaneity can be either thoughtful or thoughtless. It is a central feature of the analyst's craft to struggle with these distinctions, to make what seems to be the best choices at the time, and continually to reconsider past judgements and their sequelae, in order to expand and enrich the context in which current choices are made. (p. 146)

Mitchell's conception of Relational Psychoanalysis thus embodies elements of the interpersonal tradition with its emphasis on personal involvement and authenticity, or as he calls it, "our relational embeddedness with others." He also incorporates object relations theory with its developmental perspective "the embeddedness of others within our own minds in the internal world." Attachment theory, derived from the work of the English analyst, John Bowlby, also forms one of the foundations of Mitchell's edifice. Mitchell notes that Bowlby, viewed as an apostate by the British psychoanalytic community of his times, had to contend with the polarity between fantasy and reality. While Bowlby focused on observable behaviour, the English Kleinian analysts of his professional world were preoccupied with internal fantasy. Mitchell notes that the distinction between fantasy and reality is not drawn so sharply in current psychoanalytic theorizing, and that Fonagy (15), in particular, has examined the mental processes by which secure attachment is mediated thus opening a bridge to psychoanalytic developmental theory. Thus, incorporating aspects of attachment theory, Mitchell regards the analysts' interpretive understanding as a form of positive attachment experience. Finally, Mitchell, defines Relational Psychoanalysis as "a blending of these diverse currents into a broad, multidimensional vision of human intersubjectivity

Mitchell is careful concerning the implications of his model-building for psychoanalytic technique though he is firmly in the constructivist camp initiated by Gill:

THE EVOLUTION OF EGO PSYCHOLOGY

I divided each soul into three — two horses and a charioteer; and one of the horses was good and the other bad.
—Plato

Wallerstein, in his comprehensive review, "The Growth and Transformation of American Ego Psychology" (16), adumbrates the flowering of the metapsychological paradigm cultivated by Hartmann and his collaborators in post-World War II America. He concisely summarizes its set of constructs:

the tripartite structural model: the ego, pushed by threatened anxiety, as the mediator of the conflicting pressures of id, superego and external reality; the defensive functions of the ego; and last, the autonomous functions in an evolutionarily determined adaptation to reality, (p. 137)

This model attained in Wallerstein's words, "a monolithic hegemony over American psychoanalysis." Schafer (17) acknowledged Hartmann's brilliant efforts through this creation to bring psychoanalysis into the framework of natural science. However, fissures, even then, were already appearing in the structure. As Wallerstein notes:

Schafer could also be critical of Hartmann's thinking, in light of the explanatory paths foreclosed in this theoretical edifice, built as it was on concepts of structures and functions, forces and energies. Hartmann's conceptions clearly bypassed the ubiquitous problems of purpose, intention, and meaning that are the very essence of clinical psychoanalysis, (p. 139)

Schafer asserted that "the biological language of function cannot be concerned with meaning", an observation that had been made millennia earlier, in somewhat different words, by Aristotle.

The technical implications of Hartmann's work for the psychoanalytic situation were articulated by Eissler (18) who, closely followed an austere clinical model that had its origins in Hartmann's efforts to make psychoanalysis into an abstract general positivist psychology. Again, in Wallerstein's summary:

the hallmarks of this analytic posture were the objectivity, neutrality, abstinence, and relative anonymity of the analyst; an unremitting focus on the intrapsychic conflicts in the mind of the patient; extrusion of the personality and potentially interfering countertransferences of the analyst; and a conception of the analyst's veridical interpretations, properly reinforced through the process of working through, (p. 141)

And further: "any departure from properly timed and dosed interpretation, regarded as the only true road to insight and eventual change was labeled a 'parameter'" (p. 141).

The pejorative connotation of the appellation "parameter" is obvious, deviating as it does from "pure" analysis.

The gradual demolition of what Wallerstein calls "the ego psychology monolith" began in the 1970s. Merton Gill, who went from being an avatar of metapsychology, its codifier in his 1963 monograph, "Topography and Systems in Psychoanalytic Theory" (19), of the theory-building of Hartmann and Rapaport to the radical deconstructionist who in his 1976 paper Metapsychology is not psychology (20) sought to demolish metapsychology. His intent was to bring psychoanalytic theorizing back to an experience-near focus and away from general psychology. Gill became an ardent constructivist, an advocate of a two-person psychology at work in the clinical situation. Hoffman (21) summarizes a key element of Gill's constructivist ideas about transference and the analytic process:

The new experience associated with the analysis of the transference rests in part on the analyst's openness to the possibility that, wittingly or unwittingly, he or she has been the patient's accomplice in the perpetuation of the old, fixed patterns of interaction that the transference represents. At the very moment in which this openness is conveyed to the patient, the analyst stands a good chance of extricating himself or herself from the role of accomplice, (p. 79)

Simultaneously, Hans Loewald, while remaining within the over-arching rubric of ego psychology initiated a silent revolution with his paper "On the Therapeutic Action of Psychoanalysis" (14). Without eliciting the rancor evoked in the traditional American psychoanalysis of the time by "Kleinian" ideas, he incorporated an object-relations and developmental model into the clinical theory of ego psychology. He suggested that therapeutic effects were a consequence of ego development resuming in psychoanalysis as a result of the relationship with a new object. Loewald drew a parallel between the use of object relations in the formation and development of the psychic apparatus during childhood and the dynamics of the therapeutic process. In his view, the ego development that may take place in psychoanalysis was not simply the internalization of objects but an internalization of an interactive process between patient and analyst that included, but was not confined to, interpretive work. This was a quantum leap from Eissler's analytic 'purity' and brought the therapeutic relationship to center-stage without abandoning the precepts of ego psychology, particularly its drive theory.

Wallerstein observes that with the theoretical demise in ego psychology of energic constructs, Arlow, in a series of papers (22, 23), filled the void with his explication of the role of unconscious fantasy in psychic reality and the motivation of behavior. This was a significant advance for ego psychology and one which greatly enhanced clinical understanding and technique. He summarizes Arlow's work:

the memories that constitute our life history are created... through the mingling of external perceptions with unconscious fantasies, as experienced against the background of the individual's past development, itself a mingling of earlier perceptions and unconscious fantasies into encoded memories, (p. 157)

Gray and Busch in a series of communications (24, 25) have refined the technique of traditional ego psychology by emphasizing a focus in the clinical situation on surface meanings as a necessary prelude to interpreting underlying unconscious motivation. Brenner, in a more radical mode (26) laid a template for a new purified ego psychology in which compromise formation in response to mental conflict is dominant and omnipresent. In Brenner's view, "no aspect of ego functioning, no ego function is a 'defense mechanism.'" All aspects of ego function are "all purpose" and thus can be used in a protean manner for drive gratification, affect expression, and defensive needs depending on the nature of the conflict. Wallerstein shrewdly observes that "in the fullest extension of this thinking, Brenner seems to come close again to Hartmann's vision of a general psychology explanatory of all individual and social behaviour" (p. 159). This, of course, is a critique of the use of the philosophical doctrine of monism in psychoanalytic theorizing.

A Herculean thirty-year effort to develop an integrated ego psychology-object relations theory has been conducted by Otto Kernberg (27, 28). Kernberg was largely responsible for introducing Kleinian concepts of psychopathology into mainstream American psychoanalysis. He demonstrated the utility of Kleinian concepts, such as splitting and projective identification, in enhancing the clinical understanding of the primitive dynamics of severe personality disorders. Rigorously adhering to traditional drive theory, he has attempted to wed it to object relations theory: From a more general theoretical perspective, I believe that units constituted by a self-representation, an object representation and an affect state linking them are the essential units of psychic structure relevant for psychoanalytic exploration. Sexual and aggressive drives always emerge in the context of internalized object relations organized by affect states that, at the same time, signal these (hierarchically supraordinate) drives. To put this differently, if the only knowledge we have of drives is by their mental representations and affects, these representations are of the self and an object linked by some dominant affect state. (29, p 482)

In his integrated theory of transference, Kernberg stresses:

> that even in these relatively simple transference enactments, such activation always implies the activation of basic dyadic units of a self-representation and an object representation, linked by a certain affect which reflect either the defensive or the impulsive aspects of the conflict. More precisely, any concrete unconscious fantasy that reflects an impulse-defense organization is typically activated first in the form of the object relation representing the defensive side of the conflict and, only later, by one reflecting the impulsive side of the conflict. (29, p. 482)

The clinical implications of this model are that dominant affects, Kernberg's 'linking' mechanism, provide the key for the analyst to all interpretive work.

Another powerful current in the transformation of ego psychology has been the upsurge of interest in countertransference, not as an impediment to analysis, but as a valuable vehicle for an understanding of the patient's unconscious. This movement in American ego psychology has been promulgated by Jacobs (30) and Renik (31) who have written extensively on the use of the analyst's subjectivity as a crucial aid to analytic understanding. The Kleinian analyst Racker (32), writing in the 1960s, was crucial to this development and a number of his insightful views of transference and countertransference, shorn of Kleinian terminology, have found their way via Jacobs and others into contemporary ego psychology. Gabbard (33) has noted that the understanding of countertransference has become a consensus area among psychoanalysts of diverse theoretical perspectives. He comments that:

there is a growing recognition in all quarters that the analyst is "sucked into" the patient's world through an ongoing series of enactments that dislodge the analyst from the traditional position of the objective blank screen, (p. 77)

DISCUSSION

Hidden behind the two major movements in modern psychoanalysis of ego psychology and object relations theory lie divergent philosophical wellsprings that are not necessarily reconcilable. Modell (34) has trenchantly observed that "in a certain sense there is no such thing as a psychoanalytic theory that is accepted by a majority of psychoanalysts." To demonstrate his point, he examines three competing theories of the self promulgated by Hartmann, Winnicott, and Kohut and shows that it is impossible, given their differing philosophical premises, to incorporate them within a single model of the mind. Modell states that Hartmann's intent with his concept of "self-representation" was the objectification of subjective experience which would place the experience of the self, as an observable structure, firmly within a Cartesian system "thus contributing to the status of psychoanalysis as an 'objective' science." In contrast, Kohut's self is "a totally subjective self, a self of pure experience, known through empathy and introspection." While Winnicott shares basic philosophical assumptions with Kohut, his concept of the psychopathology of the self is different. Kohut sees pathology of the self as a function of a weakened or defective self that requires something from the outside to restore it to strength. As Modell notes, Winnicott, influenced by Fairbairn, views pathology of the self as reflecting the self being "alienated and split, retaining its potential to be healed from within." Modell further observes that these differing views lead to different therapeutic aims and that our theories do have significant practical clinical consequences.

From a philosophical viewpoint, ego psychology can be seen to have its origins in the ideas of Plato who posited a "conflict" model of the psyche in which instinctual drives (the "irrational" in Plato's terminology) represent a constant threat to rational behavior. The Platonic dialogue with its emphasis on strengthening rationality to contain the forces of irrationality find its echo in Freud's views of therapeutic action: "where id was, there shall ego be." In contrast, object relations theory can be viewed as a late flowering of the Romantic movement which promoted the primary of subjectivity and the centrality of emotional experience as a transmuting experience. The Continental European philosophy of idealism has strong affinities with the Romantic movement. Hegel is a prime exponent of this philosophy, and his work has direct links to Fairbairn and hence to Kohut. Scharff and Birtles (35) have demonstrated the influence of Hegel's Science of Logic on Fairbairn. They note that Hegel's text "is a close examination of the relationship of subject to object" and observe that "Hegel sees desire as essentially unsatisfying; where dissatisfaction leads to the need to control the object and, hence, the need to transform and own that object" ideas of pathological object relations that resurface in both Fairbairn and Kohut.

In a paper on evolving views of transference, Cooper (36) addresses the issue of the diversity of views that pervade the psychoanalytic world today. He notes that interpretation of the transference is central to all the competing psychoanalytic models.

He views the profound recent changes in definitions of transference and transference interpretation as representing a manifestation of cultural currents such as postmodernism with its switch from the diachronic position (things in their coming to be as they are) to synchrony (things as they are and ignoring how they got that way). He comments:

The transference and its interpretation are at the center of all considerations of analytic theory and technique. Freud, throughout his life, seemed astonished by the power of transference, and we are no less so. The concept was relatively simple when we understood persons as in the grip of their drives, and the purpose of the analysis was the expansion of consciousness. Today, the idea of transference has become so complex that we are no longer sure what in the analysis is not transference, and if it is not, what it is. Our loss of innocence is part of a large change in world view concerning history and truth. Major philosophical, scientific, and cultural movements, as well as our own researchers, have led to a new and desirable situation of theoretical pluralism in psychoanalysis, although at the price of the loss of a great overarching theory. As a result, our once straight-forward historical understanding of transference interpretation has yielded to a more polymorphous and confusing, but more interesting modernist view. This modernist view has raised our awareness of elements of the transference that were previously neglected, and it has opened the way for experimentation and reconsideration of many old problems, (pp. 97, 98)]

Pine (37) has attempted to deal with these apparently irreconcilable psychoanalytic philosophies by constructing what I have called a City of Psychoanalysis in which each of the major divergent theories of psychoanalysis will have a definite place and an equal prominence. Just as Augustine in his magisterial City of God provides a highly sympathetic account of the pagan philosopher Plato, Pine is sympathetic to those psychoanalytic philosophers, such as Fairbairn, Winnicott, and Kohut who deviate from the classical Freudian canon. In a series of papers and monographs, he has delineated four psychologies of psychoanalysis each to be utilized at different moments in the clinical situation.

Richards (38) however has criticized this attempt at ecumenical incorporation. He feels that Pine has been unable to overcome all the inherent difficulties in the building of an incorporative structure that provides an equal place for radically different conceptual frames. Richards observes that in his latest work, Diversity and Direction in Psychoanalytic Technique (39):

Pine specifically takes issue with the characterization of his approach as eclectic. He does so by distinguishing between "the thoughtful integrated of diverse ideas from various sources" and "a random or inconsistent or internally contradictory collection of ideas." But this attempt to differentiate "good" and "bad" forms of eclecticism does not gainsay the fact that because Pine believes that the proponents of each model can muster plausible arguments on their own behalf, the problem of establishing primacy among viewpoints becomes less urgent, (p. 16).

Ultimately, Richards is an advocate of the politics of inclusion:

Although there is much to be learned from each of these metatheories, they are all limited in various ways and present the views with which they disagree as if from the outside. Hence, rather than look to any one of them for a definitive answer, analysts should aim to steer between the Scylla of an unduly rigid insistence on antinomies and the Charybdis of a complete blurring of distinction, all the while striving to understand the subjective and ideological components of all psychoanalytic theorizing—including their own. (p. 14)

I would suggest that what we are seeing in the current theoretical ferment in psychoanalysis is the undermining by object relations theory of the classical view, which ego psychology embodies. The philosopher Isaiah Berlin (40) asserts that the occurrence of Romanticism towards the end of the 18th century was the most revolutionary of all intellectual turning points in Western history. He states:

> It seems to me, first, that certain among the romantics cut the deepest of all the roots of the classical outlook—namely the belief that values, the answers to questions of action and choice, could be discovered at all—and maintained there were no answers to some of these questions, either subjective or objective, either empirical or a priori…Thirdly, my thesis is that by their positive doctrine the romantics introduced a new set of values, not reconcilable with the old, and that most Europeans are today the heirs of both opposing traditions. We accept both outlooks, and shift from one foot to the other in a fashion that we cannot avoid if we are honest with ourselves, but which is not intellectually coherent, (p. 175)

Psychoanalysis has been an heir to the conflict that Romanticism promulgated, and it is to be found in the rise of object relations theory, intersubjectivity, and relational theories. Notwithstanding the attempts to find 'a common ground' or develop an integrated model, I concur with Modell that the fundamental conceptual frames of the two models, ego psychology and object relations theory, may well be irreconcilable in much the same way that Classicism and Romanticism cannot readily find common ground.

REFERENCES

1. Kohut, H. (1971). *The analysis of the self.* New York: International Universities Press.
2. Kohut, H. (1977). *The restoration of the self.* New York: International Universities Press.
3. Fairbairn, W.A. (1952). *Psychoanalytic studies of the personality,* London; Tavistock Publications.
4. Kohut, H. (1979). *The two analyses of Mr. Z.* International Journal of Psychoanalysis, 60, 3–27.
5. Grotstein, J.S. & Rinsley, D.B. (Eds) (1994). *Fairbairn and the origins of object relations.* New York: Guilford Press.
6. Shane, M. & Shane, E. (1993). Self psychology after Kohut: one theory or many? *Journal of the American Psychoanalytic Association,* 41, 777–797.
7. Stolorow, R. & Brandschaft, B. Atwood G (1987). *Psychoanalytic treatment: An intersubjective approach.* Hillsdale, NJ: The Analytic Press.
8. Bacal, H., & Newman, K. (1990). *Theories of object relations: Bridges to self psychology.* New York: Columbia University Press.
9. Goldberg, A. (1998). Self psychology since Kohut. *Psychoanalytic Quarterly,* 67, 240-255.
10. Dunn J (1995). Intersubjectivity in psychoanalysis: A critical review. International Journal of Psychoanalysis, 76, 723–736.
11. Jones, E. (1952). *Foreword to Fairbairn: Psychoanalytic studies of the personality. London*: Tavistock.
12. Chused, J.F. (1991). The evocative power of enactment. *Journal of the American Psychoanalytic Association,* 39, 615–640.
13. Mitchell, S.A. (2000). *Relationality.* Hillsdale, NJ & London; The Analytic Press (2000).

14. Loewald, H.W. (1980). On the therapeutic action of psychoanalysis. In *Papers on psychoanalysis*. New Haven, CT: Yale University Press.

15. Fonagy, P.. & Target, M. (1996). Playing with reality, I : Theory of mind and the normal development of psychic reality. *International Journal of Psychoanalysis, 77*, 217–233.

16. Wallerstein, R.S. (2001). The growth and transformation of American ego psychology. *Journal of the American Psychoanalytic Association, 50*, 135–169.

17. Schafer. R. (1970). An overview of Heinz Hartmann's contributions to psychoanalysis. *International Journal of Psychoanalysis, 51*, 425–446.

18. Eissler, K.R. (1953). The effect of the structure of the ego on psychoanalytic technique. *Journal of the American Psychoanalytic Association, 1*, 104–143.

19. Gill, M.M. (1963). *Topography and systems in psychoanalytic theory.* Psychological Issues Monograph 10. New York, International Universities Press.

20. Gill, M.M. (1976). Metapsychology is not psychology. In *Psychology versus metapsychology: Psychoanalytic essays in memory of George S. Klein.* Psychological Issues Monograph 36, New York, International Universities Press, pp. 71–105.

21. Hoffman, I.Z. (2000). A story in theory development in psychoanalysis. In: *Changing conceptions of psychoanalysis: The legacy of Merton M. Gill.* Hillsdale, NJ: The Analytic Press.

22. Arlow, J.A. (1969). Fantasy, memory and reality testing. *Psychoanalytic Quarterly, 38*, 28–51.

23. Arlow JA (1985). The concept of psychic reality and related problems. *Journal of the American Psychoanalytic Association, 33*, 521–535.

24. Gray, P. (1990). The nature of therapeutic action in psychoanalysis. *Journal of the American Psychoanalytic Association, 38*, 1083–1099.

25. Busch, F. (1995). Resistance analysis and object relations therapy: erroneous conceptions amidst some timely contributions. *Psychoanalytic Psychology,* 12, 43–53.

26. Brenner. C. (1982). *The mind in conflict. New* York: International Universities Press.

27. Kernberg, O.F. (1976). *Object relations theory and clinical psychoanalysis.* New York: Jason Aronson.

28. Kernberg, O.F. (1980). *Internal world and external reality: Object relations theory applied.* New York: Jason Aronson.

29. Kernberg, O.F. (1988). Object relations theory in clinical practice. *Psychoanalytic Quarterly,* 57, 481–504.

30. Jacobs, T. (1991). *The use of the self.* New York, International Universities Press.

31. Renik, O. (1996). The perils of neutrality. *Psychoanalytic Quarterly,* 65, 495–517.

32. Racker, H. (1968). *Transference and countertransference.* New York: International Universities Press.

33. Gabbard, G.O. (1995). Countertransference: The emerging common ground. *International Journal of Psychoanalysis.* 76, 475–485.

34. Modell. A. (1990). Common ground or divided ground? *Psychoanalytic Inquiry,* 14, 201–211.

35. Scharff, D.E. & Birtles, E.F. (Eds.). *From instinct to self: Selected papers of W.R.D. Fairbairn.* Northvale, NJ: Jason Aronson.

36. Cooper, A.M. (1987). Changes in psychoanalytic ideas: Transference interpretation. *Journal of the American Psychoanalytic Association,* 35, 77–98.

37. Pine, F. (1990). D*rive, ego, object, self: A synthesis for clinical work.* New York: Basic Books.

38. Richards, A.D. (1999). Brill and the politics of exclusion. Journal of the American Psychoanalytic Association, 47, 9–28.

39. Pine, F. (1996). *Diversity and direction in psychoanalytic technique.* New Haven, CT: Yale University Press.

40. Berlin, I. (1999). *The sense of reality.* New York: Farrar, Straus & Giroux.

CHAPTER 11

The Travail of David Foster Wallace : Review of " A Supposedly Fun Thing I'll Never Do Again; Essays and Arguments"

David Foster Wallace was a brilliant comic writer. Readers of this book will inevitably find themselves chortling. Wallace was also disturbing, with his mordant observations. He was illuminating in his insights concerning everyday consciousness and its flickering, malleable, nature. He was, in essence, a great artist capable of changing the reader's view of the quotidian ordinary and revealing its strangeness and beauty. Much of this was accomplished through a relentless exposure of his own anxiety-ridden subjectivity. One could speculate that he somehow retained the small child's perception of the world, one that is sometimes exhilarating, sometimes scary, and frequently fascinating. Wallace's filter for sensory experience remained porous and was vividly expressed in his writing. (I use the past tense because he committed suicide in 2008, abruptly removing himself from the stage of modem literature to which he had contributed much). The work under review is a series of essays that conform to the original meaning of the term as a literary "experiment" or "attempt." The subjects they cover are wildly disparate, ranging from Wallace's teenage experience of being a nationally ranked junior tennis player in his home state of Illinois (the reader will never feel quite the same about the Great Plains after Wallace's explication of the region's weather and geographical complexity) to a riff on late 20th-century television and its relationship to postmodernist literature to the tour-de-force, an account of a magazine-commissioned "imprisonment" of a week on a luxury cruise liner that sailed out of Fort Lauderdale through the Caribbean. In many ways, he was the penetratingly observant anthropologist, piling up reams of data, replete with exhaustive footnotes. The great Polish anthropologist, Malinowski, with his searingly self-revelatory *A Diary in the Strict Sense of the Term,* comes to mind. Wallace was the ethnographic protagonist trying to make sense out of the "alien" environments he had been sucked into. He bears comparison with Proust, another remarkable participant-observer, who was extremely funny, ironic, and poignant and was basically compassionate concerning the extravagant people he described.

Much of what is compelling about Wallace's writing is his psychic self-exposure and ongoing struggle and insights into many elements of his own mental disturbance (e.g., the crippling social anxiety, obsessive ruminations, and frank agoraphobia that beset him on the cruise ship).

Not surprisingly, Wallace's engagement with psychiatry, as both patient and caustic observer, was considerable. While an undergraduate at Amherst College, he published *The Planet Trillafon as it Stands in Relation to the Bad Thing* (1). Funny and frightening (and I suspect autobiographical), it recounts a psychotic breakdown, suicide attempt, and treatment:

'I've been on antidepressants for. what about a year now and I suppose I feel as if I'm pretty qualified to tell you what they're like. They're tine in the same way that say. living on another planet that was warm and comfortable and had food and fresh water would be fine. It would be fine but it wouldn't be good old Earth. Obviously. I haven't been on Earth now for almost a year. because I wasn't doing very well on Earth. I've been doing somewhat better here where l am now. on the planet Trillafon which I suppose is good news for everyone involved." (1, p. 26.)

In *Good Old Neon* (2), he provides a sympathetic portrait of the psychiatric treatment of a deeply disturbed narcissistic patient who perceives himself as completely empty and fraudulent. The story has a chilling outcome, presaging that of Wallace himself. In one of his master works, *Brief interviews with Hideous Men,* he includes a story titled "The Depressed Person" (3). While hilarious in parts, it is also tragic and profoundly insightful concerning affective illness, its interplay with personality disorder, and the sometimes frustrating and masochistic nature of the psychotherapeutic engagement. Wallace reveals enough knowledge about psychopharmacology and psychotherapy in this story that he could be regarded as an accomplished graduate of a very good psychiatric residency training program. He was a brilliant polymath, able to master any subject he set his mind to, including psychiatry.

Jonathan Franzen, the gifted novelist of *The Corrections,* was a close friend of Wallace. Wallace's suicide profoundly affected Franzen, and he took off for a godforsaken atoll in the South Pacific said to be where Defoe's Robinson Crusoe was marooned. There, Franzen scattered some of Wallace's ashes and came to terms with his grief and anger over his friend's suicide. His essay on this journey (4), its dangers, and his deep understanding and compassion concerning his beloved friend is almost a codicil to the book (i.e., it could have also been titled "A Fun Thing I'll Never Do Again"). Even in death, Wallace exerted a powerful influence.

REFERENCES

1. Wallace, D. (1984). The Planet Trillaphon as It Stands in Relation to the Bad Thing. *Amherst Review,* pp 26–33.
2. Wallace, D.F. (2004). Good old neon. in *Oblivion.* New York: Little Brown and Company, pp. 141–181.

3.   Wallace, D.F. (2007). The depressed person. In *Brief Interviews with Hideous Men*. New York: Back Bay: Books/Little Brown and Company, pp. 37–69.

4.   Franzen, J. (2011). Farther Away Robinson Crusoe and the Art of Solitude. *New Yorker,* April 18, 2011: pp. 80–94.

www.ingramcontent.com/pod-product-compliance
Lightning Source LLC
Chambersburg PA
CBHW062132020426
42335CB00013B/1189